LOST AND FOUND

MIKE LIPKIN

LOST AND FOUND

MY JOURNEY TO HELL AND BACK

Foreword by
Dr. Bernard Levinson

HUMAN & ROUSSEAU
Cape Town   Johannesburg   Pretoria

Except in the cases of Ogilvy & Mather, Hunt Lascaris and Grey Phillips TBWA, fictitious names have been used for advertising agencies as well as for all medical practitioners, psychiatrists and psychologists mentioned in this book.

Copyright © 1995 by Mike Lipkin
Extract from *Oh, the Places You'll Go To!* by Dr. Seuss reprinted by permission
(Copyright © 1990 by Theodor S. Geisel and Audrey S. Geisel)
First published in 1995 by
Human & Rousseau (Pty) Ltd
State House, 3–9 Rose Street, Cape Town
Cover photograph by Peter Baasch
Cover design by Etienne van Duyker
Typography by Wiekie Theron
Set in 10,5 on 13 pt Nimrod
Typesetting and reproduction by
PG&A, Ottery, Cape
Printed and bound by
National Book Printers, Goodwood

ISBN 0 7981 3406 2

To Hilary, Anthony, Carla and Dani-Emma

And to Arca Vigraha Devi Dasi – it seems like I finally learnt to listen.

If I am not for myself, who is?
If I am only for myself, what am I?
If not now, when?

ETHICS OF THE FATHERS

Foreword

He was my last patient of the evening surgery. I had never seen him before. He was not living in the False Bay area. I remember wondering why he had chosen me. The fact that he was clutching at straws – that he had, in a moment of desperation, rushed into the first doctors' surgery that was still open at that time of night, did not occur to me. He was a heavily built man in his forties, wearing a suit. His tie was undone.

Looking back on it now, I am appalled by my behaviour. The moment he started speaking, I began writing a prescription in my mind. As fast as he described a sympton, I drew out of my inexhaustible pharmacopoeia an appropriate chemical. I remember actually thinking how clever I was; how advanced we were in medicine. He couldn't sleep. In those days barbiturates were in vogue. No, not in vogue. It was all we had. I immediately planned a wise mix of intermediate and long-acting barbiturates. He had no energy. That was simple. We were blessed with stimulants, vitamins, tonics and a whole range of blunderbuss medications capable of curing everything. Cure? Well perhaps, relief . . . I wrote this pharmacological shopping list out for him on my script pad.

I was patting myself on the back when the phone rang. It was the station master of the small station across the road. Could I come quickly? Someone had fallen in front of a train. I ran, knowing with a terrible certainty what I would find. My patient was still holding my crumpled script in his hand.

"To understand others is wisdom. To understand yourself is enlightenment." How full of wisdom is this Buddhist quotation. That night I came closest to enlightenment. Under the arc lamps and amid the frantic hubbub of the police and the ambulance men, I had a moment to reflect on the sad, inept magic of my prescription. I had not really heard him. He was talking a language I had never been taught to understand. Even more basic, I had not been taught how to listen. We had missed each other completely. He was calling for help, and I was obsessed with pills. I had failed him. I had no idea what he was saying. I had the layman's concept of depression, a fleeting discomfort that will alter with circumstances. A mood. A sadness. A temporary universal experience. There was little readable literature available for professionals. There was nothing for the patient.

Mike Lipkin's vivid – painfully vivid – description of this illness, the intimate moment-to-moment flux, the bewilderment and the shattering relentless collapse of his capacity to function on every level is described with tremendous honesty and clarity. Anyone who has ever been depressed or is in the throes of a depression will feel less alone after reading this book. Being alone is what depression is all about. It's the essence of this dark illness. Burton in the 12th Century called it "the lonely night of the soul". There is no other disease that creates so powerful a sense of aloneness and helplessness. I can imagine the response of readers: "That's it! That's exactly how it was. He has found the words for me – it was like that. And he has come out of it whole and happy to be alive!"

The family of the depressed patient is also in crisis. The illness seems so inexplicable. The sudden profound dependency is practically overwhelming. How often have I heard loved ones say: "Pull yourself together!" As though the illness was within the patient's control. The patient in turn thinks: "Yes – they are right. I should pull myself together. The fact that I can't confirms how useless I am." And the symptoms get worse. How bewildering this must be for everyone!

To read this as a doctor is finally to be let into a world of suffering that still too few doctors understand. We read the journals. There is marvellous speculation about how the impulses jump from cell to cell and how our new medications change this transmission. It doesn't bring us any closer to understanding the patient. It doesn't begin to put us in touch with the agony and the despair of this illness. This is where I was as a general practitioner.

We have waited a long time for an articulate patient to take us by the hand. Depression is one of the unique areas of medicine where we have so much to learn from the patient. For the doctor who has learnt to listen it's all there, every working day of his life. The American Indians understood this when they said: "If you really want to understand me, walk in my moccasins . . ." Mike Lipkin has made it that much easier.

Bernard Levinson
Johannesburg

Contents

Prelude

What lies behind us and what lies before us, are tiny matters compared to what lies within us.

RALPH WALDO EMERSON

I am crying as I write this. Not liquid tears of self-pity, but tears of silent celebration from somewhere deep inside of me. Every day I shed these tears, every day I wake up with my senses still intact, knowing that this day brings with it a miracle. Sometimes these miracles are big and sometimes they're small. But always, they come to recharge and renew me. If you don't believe in miracles, read no further. Because miracles are what this book is all about.

Three years ago, when I was still in the demonic vice of depression, I couldn't read, I couldn't write, I could barely speak. My personality had disintegrated to the point where I had no personality. I had become that which I feared most – someone who had lost his sanity but was sane enough to know that it was lost. It was the kind of despair beyond despair. The kind of pain that still bites viciously. The kind of fear that still visits me nightly when the dreams take over.

But even then, down there in the pit where no-one should have to go, there was a part of me that dared to hope. A part of me which somehow knew that this too would pass. A part of me that was still in touch with my higher power. Like David in the Old Testament, I remember beseeching Him:

"Oh God, why hast thou forsaken me?" And so I entered into a contract with Him. If He would but give me my senses back, I would never take anything for granted again. I would worship Him every waking moment and I would help others to do the same.

The first deadly symptoms of my depressive episode manifested themselves in May 1989, a month after my thirty-first birthday. For the next three years they would spread like a mental brush fire until I was a burned-out being on the brink of suicide. Then, in February 1992, through the application of electroconvulsive therapy, they would totally disappear within seven days. What's more, I would emerge from the horror cleansed of angst and self-doubt, immunised against the disease, hopefully forever.

This book began as an article I wrote for the August 1992 issue of *Style* magazine on my struggle with the *bête noire* of depression, five months after I regained my mental health. I wrote that article as my first down payment on my contract with the Divine. It was one of the longest articles *Style* has ever run. It was also one of the most widely read. Nothing could have prepared me for the impact my story had on so many people. I was overwhelmed by the response. Within the first two months of the publication of the article, I received almost three hundred calls. A nurse from Durban reacted as strongly as a power broker from downtown Johannesburg. Letters and calls were received from all over the globe – from Cologne to Calgary to Sydney.

I think the reason why the article strongly affected so many people was that it was the first time a rehabilitated sufferer of the disease had bared his soul to other South Africans. I told my story in terms that offered empathy to anyone who had wrestled with depression. I am told that I gave hope to many readers because for the first time they realised that they were not alone. Someone else had passed through the valley of the shadow of death and come out alive, healthy, strong and maybe even more complete for having gone through the experience.

14

In October 1993, I wrote a sequel to the first article in *Style*. In the sequel, I narrated my experience of life after depression – my struggles, my realisations, my conversations with others, my beliefs and hopes. Once again, my words appear to have hit a collective chord amongst many people – the kind of people who may dare to feel more, think more, hurt more.

As you read this book, please remember that it is an account of my personal ordeal as a sufferer of clinical depression, my recovery and my realisations. It is not meant as a general medical guideline. If you have had contact with the disease, I know from the hundreds of people who have called me over the past three years that you will recognise the pain and symptoms I describe. However, individuals, circumstances and symptoms vary widely, as do successful treatments.

Obviously, the space restrictions of a magazine article limit the extent to which one can relate a story and explore its implications. This, then, is *the raison d'etre* of this book – to share with you my experience and learning. My story spans a six-year period, from 1989 to 1994. I hope it assists you in coping with the dreadful disease of depression, whether it is affecting you or someone close to you. My great wish is that the words which follow may also illuminate those miracles going on around you which may still remain camouflaged.

Just as this book is my attempt to share my experiences with you, I hope you will share your experiences with me. You can do this by writing to me c/o Lost and Found, P.O. Box 41882, Craighall, 2024. You can rest assured that no-one will see your letters but me. You will also discover, just like I did, that writing down your feelings and sharing them with another human being who empathises with you can be a powerful release from your own affliction or that of someone close to you.

I may or may not know you. But know this, I love you for your struggle. I love you for being human. I love you for your vulnerability and sensitivity. I love you for finding the determination and the desire to move forwards. Have faith, because depression is almost always beaten. All you need is the courage, the perseverance and the willingness to re-invent yourself to make it happen.

Join me now, as I take you with me on my six-year journey to hell and back.

1

The Panic

I cannot even begin to explain the nightmare I am going through with the man I've always loved and admired. Mike has just snapped. He is totally battered. He's lost his confidence and cannot think clearly. He's leaning on me for support. I am desperately trying to give it to him and yet I am struggling like hell to cope with him. He is demotivated to work. Can you imagine that?!!! He has no enthusiasm to read. Can you believe that?!!! He won't run or take care of himself. He frightens me beyond conceivable thought. I have to believe he'll sort himself out, otherwise we're all goners. It's like it's all been too perfect for us. Yikes, it's rough.

HILARY LIPKIN'S DIARY, 28 JUNE 1989

It felt like a mental heart attack, hitting me with such force that I was physically winded. Someone or something was cannibalising me from within. As I gasped for air, I knew that the fear which had been gestating over the previous five weeks had finally given birth to full-blown panic.

It was 8 p.m. on Friday 28 June 1989. I was in my office at Ogilvy & Mather, Toronto – one of Canada's leading advertising agencies. I was surrounded by the accoutrements of my achievements over the past two years – the big corner office, the leather suite, the framed Matisse prints and photos of magic moments on the wall, the panoramic view of downtown Toronto. I had made it to the top of the advertising industry in my adopted country. I had realised my dream just as it turned to dread.

Although the office was air-conditioned, the sweat began to ooze out of me. It felt as if my mind was bleeding. I stood up and began to pace the room, clenching and unclenching my fists. I had never experienced such negative intensity of emotion. My adrenaline surged, but instead of the usual rush of exhilaration, the terror became almost tangible. I remember thinking: "Thank God everyone has gone home." Over the previous few weeks, I had managed to disguise the fear circling my psyche like some ugly predator. But now it had me in its rabid embrace and I could pretend no more.

I stayed in the office for another hour, locked in a state of agitated paralysis. The ashtray was crammed with the stubs of the full packet of cigarettes I had smoked since returning from my last meeting at 6 p.m. I knew that I had to go home to my worried wife, Hilary, but I couldn't face the one-hour journey to my house. Even the most routine activity now filled me with anxiety. I couldn't even call her to tell her I would be late. She was aware of my deteriorating state. I knew she would ask me how I felt and I knew my voice would betray me.

"This can't be happening, this can't be happening, this *can't* be happening," I chanted silently as I paced up and down my luxurious cell. I had always been in control of my situation and my emotions. My ability to thrive in even the most daunting circumstances had become my trademark characteristic. "I am at my best when things are at their worst" was the one belief that had sustained me my entire adult life. I grimaced as I considered the bizarre irony of my current condition: I was at my worst when things were at their best, when all my aspirations had been realised.

A knock on the door disturbed my agonised reverie. "Oh shit," I mumbled, abruptly aware of my dishevelled state, "who the hell can this be?" I opened the door to discover the night cleaning lady. "I clean office, okay?" she said, smiling, in her broken English. As she entered, I was struck by the difference between us. I guessed that she was a Filipino immigrant, in her mid-twenties. With minimum skills, she was working for minimum wage. In all likelihood, she was working both day and night to survive. And yet there was no trace of bitterness or resignation about her. She went about her work with a conscientious efficiency that filled me with a weird sense of envy. Despite her circumstances, she was *coping* with life. I wasn't.

It was 9 p.m. I couldn't procrastinate any longer so I headed home. As I stepped outside the building I inhaled the mild night air of early summer. I had always loved this time. The end of a long, hard day's work. The anticipation of the 45-minute train ride to the final stop where I would take the bus to my house. Inevitably, I would doze off on the train, waking up refreshed for the couple of hours' work I would do every night. Five weeks previously, I would have been filled with a sense of complete wellbeing. Now I was consumed with absolute fear and self-doubt.

I descended into the subway and boarded the train. I glanced around me. Although it was late, the train was more than half full. I marvelled at the diversity of people on the train. Toronto is a city of immigrants with one of the biggest populations in the world of Greeks, Italians, Jamaicans, Filipinos, Chinese and South Africans outside of their native countries. I had loved being one of these immigrants, starting from scratch to re-invent the future – a future that had suddenly turned rotten.

My restlessness prohibited me from sitting still. Unconsciously, I began to rock in my seat and wring my hands. I rubbed my sweaty palms together, ran them through my hair and then wiped them on my jacket. I stood up and walked to another seat and then another, driven by a distress that seemed to worsen with every passing kilometre. I became aware of the stares of my fellow passengers. It was a look that I would become used to over the next three years; the kind of look that a sane person gives to a person who has been touched by the wing of madness.

Eventually, the train reached the end of the line. I went immediately to the nearest shop and bought my third packet of cigarettes for the day. I knew I was poisoning myself, but at least the act of lighting and smoking a cigarette provided some outlet for the exploding emotions within. I smoked compulsively for a few moments and then flicked the cigarette away as I saw the number 7 bus to Thornhill, the suburb where we lived, enter the station.

My sense of desperation mounted during the brief bus ride to our house. It was now past 10 p.m. It had been fifteen hours since I left home at 7 a.m. that morning. The only food I had eaten was a hot dog purchased from a street vendor at lunch time. I didn't know it at the time, but I was experiencing my first taste of the lethal torture that is a common symptom of severe depression – the malicious combination of extreme exhaustion and neurotic nervousness. I would discover that there is no rest for the wicked or the severely depressed.

I got off the bus at the stop about 400 metres from our house. As I walked slowly towards it, I knew that the torment that had engulfed me for the past four hours was just the foreplay to what was coming. It was one thing writhing in private pain. Inflicting another person with it would be pure hell. As I opened the door, I saw Hilary standing there in her pyjamas, almost childlike. Until that moment I had attempted to hide my disintegration from her. She had noted the telltale signs of my self-neglect. I had stopped running, which was almost a religious regimen of mine. I had stopped reading, which was my passion. I spent far less time on my grooming. I had lost interest in exploring the countryside around Toronto during our frequent weekend trips. In short, I had begun to hate everything I used to love. But at least I retained some semblance of normality. I was still a good father. I was still a reasonably social being. My libido still sustained a satisfying sexual relationship. "It's just a phase he's going through," she rationalised to herself. "Everyone goes through it at one point or another," her friends and family told her, "he'll get over it."

But the moment we looked at each other that night, we knew instinctively that I had been gripped by a pathology that would not just blow over. His eyes are dead, Hilary thought, he looks as if he's become unravelled from the inside out. Suddenly she understood with a chilling clarity that something in our lives had been broken. But that night neither of us could have anticipated the pain to come, and so her naive optimism remained intact.

She approached me with a mixture of trepidation and tenderness. Gently, she laid her hand on my arm and stroked me. As I saw the look of puzzlement and pain in her eyes, I stepped back as though I were allergic to her touch. With a shock, I realised I was ashamed. I was out of control. I was falling apart when my role was to hold everything together. I did not feel worthy of her act of kindness. I did not feel as if I deserved her esteem. As her husband, it had taken me seven years to become her rock. It took me just one day to crumble.

"Talk to me," she said despairingly, but I just turned away and went upstairs. How could I explain something to her that was so beyond my own comprehension? As I turned to enter our bedroom, I looked down the passageway to where our twin children, Carla and Anthony, were sleeping. They were five years old. I have no right to surrender to my weakness like this, I thought: those two little people are depending on me. But instead of rallying me, the responsibility washed over me in a wave of nausea. If I couldn't even take care of myself, how was I going to take care of them?

I peeled off my clothes and went into the bathroom. As I looked at the face in the mirror, I felt an alien sense of duality. It was as if Mike Lipkin had fragmented into two selves – the physical incarnation whose reflected image stared back at me, and another disembodied self, detached from reality, who was rational and collected. What was really happening, I discovered later, was that my reason and emotions had taken leave of each other. My reason told me that I should be celebrating life. It told me that whatever the challenges confronting me, they were *well* within my capability to master them. Emotionally, though, I felt as though I had stepped into a quicksand of fear whose vortex threatened to swallow me completely.

I looked at that face with a mounting sense of loathing as the sound of Hilary's muted sobs slapped me. What's wrong with you? the voice lambasted me. What are you made of? How selfish can you be? Can't you hear Hilary crying? Don't you owe it to her to snap out of it? You can't afford the luxury of feeling sorry for yourself! Don't throw it all away now, pal. Don't you realise what's at stake here? Or are you just chicken? This ain't no game! "I know, I know," I shouted silently, crippled by confusion. I felt the urge to vomit and shit at the same time. My mind and body seemed to be unravelling simultaneously.

The first signs of the psychosis that would eventually envelop me entirely had begun to manifest themselves. Until the first attack in my office earlier that evening, I had never experienced the shock of full-blown panic. I had felt scared; I had felt overwhelmed; I had felt uncertain; I had felt uncomfortable; for brief moments, I had even felt unable to cope. But never this sense of utter helplessness. And so I continued with my chant of denial: "This can't be happening, this can't be happening, this *can't* be happening."

I stepped into the bath and tried to still the thoughts ricocheting around my mind. Just calm down, I said to myself in vain as I immersed myself in the water, at least it's the weekend. You've got two days to pull yourself together before going back to work on Monday. I lay there for a long time trying to summon back my sanity. But then, as I submerged my head, I fantasised about oblivion for the first time. It seemed like the only escape from this cerebral cyclone. Over the next three years, this fantasy would become an increasingly enticing option.

It was now 12.15 a.m. Although the lights had been turned off in the bedroom, I could see that Hilary had gone to bed. I went downstairs, feeling light-headed from lack of food. But I wasn't hungry. My stomach seemed to have contracted into a lead ball. I opened the cabinet and reached for the Scotch. I poured myself over half a glass, lit a cigarette and turned on the TV. I knew I had to prevent myself from thinking. If I couldn't do it on my own, I would do it with the help of alcohol, nicotine and the flickering screen in front of me. As I sat there, despite the torment, I did not consciously regard myself as *sick*. Antidepressants and psychotherapy were still way beyond my frame of reference.

The double dose of whisky and cigarette on an empty stomach had its desired effect. The jagged edges of my shattered mind were smoothed. The voice in my head fused with the voices of the celluloid figures in front of me. I was in nowhereland, bathed in numbness of mind and body. At last, I could succumb to the arms of Morpheus.

2

The Fairy Tale

It was 12 April 1982. I had just walked into the Grey Advertising offices in Rosebank, Johannesburg, for a job interview. I was almost 24 years old. Although I had never been there before, I felt at home. The wall-to-wall mirrors, the receptionist who looked as if she had ordered her face from *Vogue* magazine, the designer furniture, the people running to and fro with their layout boards under their arms – this was the stuff of which my dreams were made.

Ever since I could remember, I had wanted to be an adman. Advertising is the art form of business. It's an industry whose stock in trade is ideas, words and pictures. Products are made in a factory, but images are made in an ad agency. And it's the images which sell. The best ad agencies are really dream merchants. That's why there is a sense of unreality about them. They are one step removed from the grey realities that define most other businesses. I knew instinctively that I belonged in this world of make-believe.

Everything I had achieved until that moment said to the world that I was smart. I did well at school. I thrived at university where I had earned a B. Comm. Honours degree in Marketing. Concurrently, I ran a small direct-selling business which made me self-sufficient by the age of eighteen. I excelled at my first job as a product manager at Colgate Palmolive. I had a flawless CV. I was the quintessential overachiever addicted to the narcotic of success. It wasn't the money that was so seductive, but the adulation of my family and friends. And yet somehow, even then, it was never enough. The more I achieved, the greater the drive became. It was as though I was shadowed by a bogeyman who threatened to take it all away unless I pushed myself harder and harder.

The interview went smoothly. I got the job as a trainee account executive, the person who liaises between the client and the ad agency. The adventure that was to end almost fatally had begun.

The next few years were the most exhilarating of my life. Someone once said that advertising is the most fun you can have with your clothes on. And it's true. If you are endowed with chutzpah, charisma and imagination, together with a deep reservoir of resilience and stamina, advertising is the only game in town. With the wonderfully naive arrogance of youth, I believed I had all those qualities in abundance.

Luck and timing were on my side. I joined Grey Phillips just as their halcyon years started. The agency's growth exploded and so did my career. My energy and drive, which I realise now was manic in its intensity, catapulted me to the top. In just four years I graduated from being a trainee account executive to senior client service director and member of the board. I became the protégé of the chairman, Darryl Phillips. Together, we would sit in his epicurean eyrie discussing strategy and ways of stealing business from our competitors, unaware that the hubris we were displaying would be our downfall.

I did not know it at the time, but the trouble was that I began to believe my own hype. I became a master mimic, aping the style and gestures of the powerful, rich and famous. There was no real Mike Lipkin. Rather, I was a walking composite of other people's personalities. But I had learnt my lessons well. Like the products I advertised, I had crafted an alluring image for myself that exuded self-assurance. By all external measures, I was a winner. And in business, people love being with a winner. An insistent instinct warned me that this charade was unsustainable. I ignored it. I was 28 years old. I was fooling all of the people all of the time. I was happy, or so I thought.

At the beginning of 1986, Darryl Phillips left for the UK to begin a business there. That March, he asked me to come to Leeds, in the north of England, to manage a small ad agency he was considering acquiring. After close scrutiny, we decided against the purchase, but I had been exposed to the international arena. I had proven that I could be a champion in South Africa. I felt I had outgrown the local marketplace. Now, I wanted to see whether I could cross swords with the best the world had to offer.

We decided to emigrate to Toronto, Canada. It seemed like the logical destination. It was a world-class city and the country's commercial engine, with a thriving advertising community. It was only 500 km from New York to the east and Chicago to the west. With a population of almost 50 000 ex-South Africans, including my wife's two sisters, it also offered us a family to replace the one we were leaving behind.

It was relatively easy to obtain the Canadian "green card". In 1986, North America was booming. Demand for immigrants with advertising and marketing skills had hit an all-time high. In addition, Hilary was a qualified speech therapist – another occupation in great demand. We were in our late twenties. We had money. We were the perfect immigrant family. I remember feeling like Columbus. Canada was the brave new world and I was going to conquer it.

From Johannesburg, I applied to 22 Toronto ad agencies, including one of the world's top global agencies, Ogilvy & Mather. Of all the agencies I applied to, Ogilvy & Mather was the only one to respond to my fax. They stated that they would be delighted to meet with me and that they had a possible opportunity. My fellow South Africans who had worked there before me had established a proud tradition. They were known for their boldness, work ethic and bias towards action. My life was a fairy tale. I could see the yellow brick road stretching indefinitely into the future.

I flew across to Toronto to get the job, find a house and lay the foundation for my family who would follow later. I arrived in Toronto in the middle of summer. The temperature was 36 degrees Celsius, with 95 percent humidity. It made Durban feel like the Sahara. As I emerged from the airport terminal, I felt as if I had just stepped into a plate of soup. But then my adrenaline began to pump as I travelled down the six-lane highway to my sister-in-law who lived in Thornhill, the South African Jewish ghetto, an upmarket neighbourhood about 25 kilometres north of downtown Toronto.

The immediate impression a Johannesburger has of Toronto is that it is impossibly clean and well ordered. *Time* magazine called it "New York run by the Swiss". It is also a very new city with much of its development having taken place over the past two decades. However, in the residential areas, most of the houses are precisely the same – prescription buildings constructed from a common blueprint. In Toronto, only the super-rich can afford to design their own homes. The immediate adjustment for a South African, though, is that there are no walls or fences and the plots are minute, even in the most affluent areas.

Over the next three weeks I found a place to rent, opened a bank account and snared the job at Ogilvy & Mather, situated in the heart of Toronto's business centre. I went through a series of interviews with the agency's management, culminating in a final meeting with the chairman. He offered me a position far below the one I occupied in South Africa. My immediate response was disappointment, and my expression mirrored my chagrin. I know now that very often a person's greatest strength is his or her greatest weakness. I was powered by an acute sense of urgency. In the past, I had always accelerated the natural pace of progress. Impatience had become ingrained in my character.

The chairman, himself an immigrant from Britain, was an astute reader of people. He warned me that Canada had very little tolerance for people with impatience and ambition. He said, and I'll never forget these words: "Canadians gang up on those who express their ambitions too blatantly." He told me that this wasn't America, the land of the free and the brave, where the cowboy was the national icon and the three fundamental tenets of the constitution were "life, liberty and the pursuit of happiness".

This was Canada, where the Mounty reigned and the cornerstones of the constitution were "peace, order and good government". Coming from the boom or bust mining-town mentality of Johannesburg, I didn't listen to him. It was a deafness that would cost me dearly.

And so, at the beginning of 1987, we flew to Toronto. It seemed different to Johannesburg in every way. Toronto was the darling of the international investment community with its internal social stability, low inflation rate, almost universally literate adult population and proximity to the US market. Crime was almost nonexistent. Social services like medical care were among the most developed in the Western world. At the same time, however, there was a price to pay for all this order. After the dusty drama of the Highveld, Canada was bland. It had the flavour of vanilla and the texture of white bread. What the hell, I thought. Here I am in the fifth largest city in North America. I'm young. I've got a job with a blue-chip company. I'd find a way to make the country work for me.

I attacked my job with the explosion of energy that had become my trademark. Ogilvy & Mather was the IBM of the local advertising community. The fundamental operating principle enshrined in the agency's mission statement was: "First-class business in a first-class way". But Ogilvy & Mather was also an ad agency which had gone stale. It lacked the entrepreneurial hustle that characterised the hot, new, smaller agencies invading the marketplace. At Grey Phillips in South Africa, though, we were the champions of hustle. It was the overriding feature of our corporate culture. And so, the chairman of Ogilvy & Mather made me the unofficial agent of change. I was encouraged to do and say the things he couldn't or wouldn't do and say. At the same time, my clients lauded my contribution to their business.

The fabulously familiar pattern began to reassert itself. Within nine months, I was promoted to the position I had held in South Africa, becoming one of the youngest client service directors in Ogilvy & Mather Canada's history. An associate of mine was appointed president of BMW Canada and he asked me to do consulting work for him. I also identified the opportunity to work with some of my ex-South African clients, where I would provide them with a North American perspective on their businesses.

We established a strong social network within the closely knit South African community. Soon I was consulting for a number of companies run by ex-South Africans. The fairy tale continued. I had hit the ground running and it all seemed to come so naturally to me. Although the landscape had changed, the principles of business remained precisely the same. The level of expertise and pace of Grey Phillips in South Africa, combined with the exhilaration of making my mark in one of the biggest advertising markets in the world, empowered me to do more and more. I found myself working sixteen hours a day, six days a week. And always, I was spurred by my old partner, the bogeyman of urgency, who became even more powerful because I knew that there was no safety net to catch me if I stumbled.

I began to mainline on the euphoria of achievement. I became a recognition junkie. The more outrageous and flamboyant my operating style and ideas became, the more successful I was. It is an extraordinary advantage being a South African within Canadian culture. Canadians who play by the rules of convention. However, if you are a successful immigrant, you are granted immunity from these rules – *provided you are successful.* In hindsight, I believe I was nothing more than a curiosity to my Canadian counterparts. I think they used to vicariously enjoy my extrovert nature and uninhibitedness because their internal code of conduct prohibited them from being the same. But God help you if you flouted the rules and failed – as I was about to find out.

By the spring of 1989, two years after we arrived in Canada, I was at the apex of my career. I was making more money than I ever believed possible. My wife had established a thriving private speech-therapy practice. I felt we could do no wrong.

We were living in a tiny house in Thornhill which we had bought within seven days of arriving in Canada. I had followed the advice of a mentor of mine from Johannesburg who advised me to buy the smallest house in the best neighbourhood. But now, with my meteoric career and earnings rise, I began to lust after a grander residence – one that would truly broadcast my achievements to the world.

3

The Trigger

Well, we're heading quickly towards the end of 1989. Mike's condition is no better. In fact, it seems even worse. It seems like we've been living in this dark hole for ages. It's like he's going through a meltdown. All he can speak about is the damn house. It's such a trauma for me to watch this young dynamic man crumble like he is. I have to believe that he'll have the strength to rebuild. I love him and yet I am feeling such hate towards him right now. I can only pray and support him as much as possible. I am feeling such anxiety, such apprehension and such an overwhelming feeling of helplessness and loss. All I desire now is to feel the strength and emotional security I used to feel with Mike. Please God let everything be OK. The kids are my saviour.

HILARY LIPKIN'S DIARY, 28 July 1989

12 March 1989 was the day I pulled the trigger. It was one of those magnificent Canadian spring Sundays. The sky was a flawless blue. The freshly fallen snow almost glowed with the reflected rays of a sun that had emerged for the first time in weeks. The air was cold and crisp, gently nipping my throat as I inhaled. Even our dog Babyface, a mongrel mix of poodle and spaniel, seemed to sense the magic of the moment. I had finished my work for the weekend and I was revelling in the sheer ecstasy of being alive. I remember the scene so graphically because it was the last time for three

years that I would feel truly content and in control of my life.

Hilary rushed into our little back garden, still flushed from the aerobics class she had just given. "I've found it," she shouted, "the house of our dreams." Although I had no specific plans to buy another house, I was infected by her excitement. Later that afternoon, I went with her to see it. It was beautiful. Set on a huge piece of land by Toronto standards, it even had a swimming pool, a big indulgence in a country that only offered eight to ten weeks of swimming weather a year. Inside, it was spacious and well appointed. But I didn't see bricks and mortar or the financial implications of buying the house – all I saw was the perfect expression of my achievements. As I stood there on the patio, looking out over the garden and then back into the lounge, I visualised the hordes of clients I would host in this monument to myself.

Although I heard a small but insistent voice warning me against doing what I was about to do, I heard my other voice saying to the real estate agent: "We like it. I think we'll take it." Five hours later, with less thought than I would give to buying a chocolate bar, I had spent almost C$500 000 (R1,3 million) on something I really didn't need.

Fate can be a cruel thing. I had made the cardinal error of buying before selling our existing house. Four days after we had signed the unqualified purchase agreement, the interest rate rose by two percentage points. The booming Toronto real-estate market collapsed overnight as the overheated Canadian economy began the spiral that is still continuing. I couldn't sell our existing house, which we were counting on doing to partially finance the new one.

My unbroken series of home runs at work came to an end as my clients started preparing for the long recession that lay ahead. I had severely underestimated the stress of operating in a sliding economy. All of a sudden, my clients were not embracing my aggressive ideas with the same affection. Now I imagined I saw only suspicion on their faces. Their emphasis had shifted from the accelerator to the brake. After two years in the country, I thought I had developed an intimate understanding of the Canadian psyche. The truth is, I hadn't even begun to understand it. I had been too preoccupied with my own quest for glory.

Although we purchased the house in March, we were only scheduled to move in at the beginning of June. Three months is a long time to sell our existing house, I tried to reassure myself unconvincingly. The whole of March passed, then April, then May. We didn't receive so much as a nibble. It became clear that I had made a huge mistake. I was calling the real-estate agent six times a day. No matter where I was or what I was doing, I would phone her, as if by sheer persistence I would force her to sell the house. Eventually, in desperation, she called Hilary. "I'm worried about your husband's mental health," she said. "He can't understand that there's nothing more I can do. Give your house to someone else to sell. I can't handle him anymore." Hilary pacified her and pleaded with me to stop the craziness. But the more I thought about it, the more alarmed I became. Darryl Phillips or the chairman of Ogilvy & Mather would never have made this mistake, I ruminated, opening the floodgates of self-doubt.

"You can fool everyone else, but you can't fool yourself," the voice told me. "You see, you're really not that smart. In fact, you're nothing but an imposter," my negative self-talk continued. I had always believed that there was no life after debt. Yet, in one devastating move, I had accumulated debt beyond my wildest dreams. We failed to sell our existing house before moving into the new one. My monthly mortgage repayments ballooned past R10 000. The fixation with debt blurred my focus at work. My head became filled with static. I began to ask myself questions I had never asked before: "What if I fail? What if I lose my job? What if I can't pay the mortgage? What if they all discover that I'm really just a fraud?" The bogeyman was becoming real and he was taking over. It felt as if I was playing the lead role in some ludicrous melodrama, except that the melodrama was real and it was happening to me.

The tragicomedy took a twisted turn during our first night in the new house. I had long given up hope of ever again enjoying the simple pleasure of uninterrupted, unassisted sleep. At about 3 a.m., after a couple of hours of fitful dozing in my sweat-drenched sheets, the walls began to shake to the sound of a locomotive that seemed to be travelling through our back yard. I sat bolt upright, uncertain whether my mind was playing tricks on me or whether the sound was real. But as I sat there wide awake, the sound continued, growing louder and louder. It must have lasted for a full five minutes. The following day I discovered to my chagrin that a railway line lay about a hundred metres from the house, behind our neighbours on the other side of the street. I hadn't seen it because it was shaded by a row of maple trees. I took it as just one more sign that the entire universe was conspiring against me.

On 15 June, I received a call from the real-estate agent. "I've found you a buyer," she said. "He's put in a firm offer. It's below the price you wanted but under the circumstances, I think it's a damn good deal." That night, we sold the house. My mortgage was reduced to C$220 000 (R550 000), still much larger than it was before we bought the new house but not alarming by Toronto standards. I should have been delighted. Despite my self-doubt, however, I continued to cope at work. Together with Hilary's income and the dividends we were still receiving from our South African investments, we easily covered the mortgage payments. But the incorrigible fear inside me continued growing until that evening on 28 June when it exploded into panic.

On the morning of 29 June 1989, the sun rose as it always does. But I cursed the light which forced me to confront myself again. I craved the darkness. At night, I could wrap the blackness around me like a blanket and disembody myself. At night, the birds didn't sing and mock me with their cheerfulness. At night, I could hide.

The frantic panic of the evening before had congealed into a tension that froze me. I felt paralysed from the mind down.

I was afraid to move, as if any motion would plunge me back into turmoil. My regret was rampant. I was obsessed about the mistake I had made with the house. The object of desire had become an object of loathing, exacerbated by the fact that I had spent C$500 000 to torture myself. The events of 12 March played themselves over and over again in my mind. The more I thought about that day, the more shocked I was about my lapse of judgement. I was terrified that my thirty-one-year-old winning streak had been abruptly terminated. My warped logic told me that winners don't screw up the way I did. I was convinced that my past success was merely a mirage. From that point on, I was a loser.

"Daddy!" The sound ripped into me. My little girl shouted with delight as she bounded into the room and saw me on the couch. "Look what I made for you at school to put on your wall at work," she said, holding up a drawing. "That's you holding Anthony's hand and that's Mommy holding my hand. And there's Babyface." She stood there expectantly, waiting for the usual expression of effusive praise. But all I could muster was a flat "very nice". "Don't you like it?" she asked, puzzled by my lack of response. I was stabbed with guilt. Enthusiasm had been erased from my repertoire of emotions. I sat up and hugged her. "I'm so sorry," was all I could say to myself.

It was 10 a.m. The smell of pancakes and freshly brewed coffee wafted into the lounge. Breakfast of pancakes and coffee was our weekly Saturday ritual. It was always a special time, the beginning of the weekend where we sat down as a family and planned our activities for the next couple of days. But not this morning. Hilary glanced at me nervously as if she was afraid to look at me. I barely greeted her as I sat down at the table. I knew I had to eat but everything tasted bland, and I consumed my food mechanically. It was as though my chaotic mental state had corrupted all my other senses. A pall of silence settled over us. Even the children became quiet, their natural ebullience smothered by the bizarre behaviour of their father.

"I was so worried about you, I called Ian," Hilary said with a strained voice. Ian was our family doctor and friend. "He's coming to see you. Maybe he can help you." Although I was nonplussed by my affliction, Hilary suspected that I was in the grip of depression. As she would do increasingly in the months ahead, she had assumed the initiative. I couldn't see how a doctor was going to help me. I wasn't physically ill. I had become mentally unstuck. There was no antibiotic for regret or loss of self-confidence, I thought. Instead, I felt embarrassed. Until then, only Hilary and I knew of my distress. As far as the rest of the South African community was concerned, I was still a success story. I was Ian's friend, not his patient. Instead of gratitude, I felt an absurd surge of anger towards Hilary. Now everyone would find out that I was really a loser.

"Tell him not to come!" I shouted, feeling my emotions start to boil again. "I don't want him to see me like this. I'm in shit, but it's my problem. I'll sort it out." I turned on her and yelled accusingly "First you make me buy a house that we don't need. Then you embarrass me in front of my friends. It's all your fault. How dare you call Ian without speaking to me!" Suddenly, I began to choke with rage. I picked up a glass and hurled it against the wall. Then I turned around and punched the wall behind me. I heard a knuckle crack as my fist went through the board. But I welcomed the pain. I wanted to hurt myself. The wide-eyed stare of my twins as they clutched their mother heightened my self-hate. That's when the doorbell rang.

Hilary took the children with her as she opened the door. I heard her break down in tears as she saw Ian. He came into the kitchen, clearly astonished by what he saw. The shattered glass on the floor, the hole in the wall, the terrified twins standing by the door and me standing there, holding my right hand to my stomach in pain. I saw him retreat into his professional shell. His voice assumed the arm's-length tone of doctor to patient. "Come and sit down," he said gently, as he guided me into the lounge. From his telephone conversation with Hilary, he knew about my collapse over the past twelve hours. But the scene that confronted him convinced him I was in crisis.

"Hilary told me about your agitation," he said with monumental understatement. "Could you describe your feelings for me?" At first, I held back. My outburst had stunned me. I felt like Jekyll and Hyde, oscillating wildly between anger and anxiety. Then I began to talk. I told Ian about the relentless panic, the inability to think about anything else but the house, the loss of self-confidence and the sense of self-shame. But I kept coming back to the house and the mortgage as the reason why I was disintegrating.

Ian shook his head and said to me: "Mike, I promise you it's not the house. I know lots of people who've made a mistake in buying a house. I understand that you're upset about the drop in the market and the size of your mortgage. But let me tell you, my mortgage is even bigger than yours and I'm not earning anywhere near the kind of money you're earning. Everyone in this city is in hock up to their ears. Canada is a country built on debt. Welcome to the real world. The house was just the trigger. I have to tell you that I think you may be suffering from an acute depressive episode. It's as much a sickness as flu or pneumonia and it can become very serious if you don't get the proper treatment. I'm going to refer you to a psychiatrist, Dr Haines, and I'll make sure he sees you on Monday morning. In the meantime, I'm going to prescribe a tranquilliser to help you stay calm and get some sleep." He wrote out a prescription and then rose to leave. "Don't worry, it will be okay," he said, but his eyes said something very different.

I felt an odd sense of relief. I was sick, that's why I was acting so strangely. I would get help. I would be okay.

If only it had turned out to be so simple.

4

Into the Pit

It's 1.15 am and I feel as though I am about to burst with such sadness and total bereavement. Michael, it seems, has lost the will to fight this consuming mental anguish. I feel like he has died. My whole life is about to change if I do not take control of myself and the kids. I too will become ill. I feel so hatefully morbid that I'm beginning to doubt my own sanity. I feel as though I've been taken from an enchanted garden and dipped over and over again in tar. I am sadly coming to the realisation that I will not be able to respect him the way I used to. Every minute, every second, he belittles himself. He has no self-worth whatsoever. It is so incredibly hard for me because he has always been my emotional stronghold. This fort of power and energy. Oh how I miss him. He doesn't talk and when he does, it's only about what he had and what he's lost. I am so tired of crying and this constant nagging torment. It's so sad that he's chosen to behave in this revolting mindless way. Only a miracle, it seems, will be able to reunite this team that could continue to be unbeatable. But he won't allow that to happen. I am so filled with rage and disrespect. Do I still love him? I don't think I do. There is too much discolouration. I doubt whether the clouds hanging over us will ever be lightened or erased.

HILARY LIPKIN'S DIARY, 10 AUGUST 1989

Monday morning, 1 July 1989. I called Ogilvy & Mather to tell them I was sick and that I wouldn't be coming in that day.

My secretary expressed her sympathy and then asked the dreaded question: "What's wrong?" I smiled grimly to myself. I could imagine her response if I said: "Well, it seems like I'm suffering from acute depression and I'm on my way to see a psychiatrist so he can treat me before my condition worsens." So all I told her was that I was running a fever and that I was going to see the doctor.

We sat in silence as Hilary drove me to the psychiatrist. It was now impossible for me to sit still. It was as though a thousand spiders were crawling just beneath my skin, causing me constant discomfort. I writhed and rocked in my seat, imprisoned in my misery. "Why, why, why," was the only word reverberating in my head. Why the hell did I buy the house? Why wasn't I satisfied with what I had? Why was I so scared? I would learn later that the obsession with a phantom predicament was just one more hallmark of my condition.

Dr Haines's rooms were located in a nondescript building on the corner of Bay and Dundas streets in midtown Toronto. As we waited in the reception area, I kept on thinking that life wasn't supposed to turn out this way. This was not my destiny. Mike Lipkin was not meant to be mentally ill. I was meant to be in a boardroom, championing deals, pioneering breakthrough ways of doing business, not sitting vegetable-like, waiting in fear to see a psychiatrist. A psychiatrist! Like most other so-called healthy people, I believed psychologists and psychiatrists were only there for the weak and those unable to cope with life. I had always believed I was bulletproof. For the first time, I realised with a shock just how fragile my ego really was.

Dr Haines came out to greet us, carrying a clipboard. He looked as if he had just stepped out of a Hollywood soap opera. He was taller than I was, over six feet. I guessed he was in his early fifties. His thick, black hair was laced with silver. He wore horn-rimmed glasses and a tweed jacket with leather patches at the elbows. He had the look of a man who lived his life in the middle of the comfort zone. "Michael and

39

Hilary Lipkin?" he enquired, as he looked at us. We nodded. "Please follow me," he said as he turned and walked back to his office. Immediately, I knew he had put a distance between us. There was no handshake, no reassuring smile: even his voice was impeccably neutral.

His office looked like a movie set. It was a perfect replica of the celluloid version – the subdued browns, the book-lined wall, the leather couch facing two easy chairs. Even the silence had the quality of an anaesthetic about it. It was an insulated chamber protected against the hurly and burly of the real world. He appeared to consult his notes and then, peering over his clipboard, he asked Hilary to tell him what had happened. Hilary told him about my self-erosion over the previous three months since the purchase of the house, culminating in my aberrational behaviour over the week-end. "Has this ever happened before?" he asked, directing his question again at Hilary. I realised that he was trying to get an objective view of the situation, not my attenuated interpretation of events. "Never," Hilary replied, "and that's what makes it so hard for me to understand. I don't think he was ever down for longer than a few hours before. And even then, it was nothing like this." Dr Haines scribbled something down and then turned his expressionless attention to me.

"Tell me what you're feeling," he said. This time, the words came pouring out of me in a haphazard rush. I told him about my extraordinary performance since we had arrived in Canada. I described how much I loved achievement and recognition. But then I found myself dwelling on my enigmatic sense of loss – the loss of my energy, my *joie de vivre*, my enthusiasm, my self-pride. "That damn house is sucking the lifeblood out of me," I said. Even as I was telling my story, though, it sounded ludicrous. I felt as if I was drowning in self-pity.

Dr Haines reaffirmed Ian's prognosis: "Michael, the house is just a parachute," he said. "It's the external reason you are applying to what's going on here." He pointed to his head.

40

"From what Ian has told me and our discussion here this morning, I think you are suffering from clinical depression. It's nothing to be ashamed of. It's a disease that is as much physical as it is mental. Did you know that at least ten percent of Canadian adults will experience a severe depression during their lifetime, although the vast majority recover to lead perfectly normal lives? Furthermore, depression is completely democratic. It hits people of any age, race, occupation or income group. But whether you were aware of it or not, people like you are particularly vulnerable to this disease." I shook my head in disbelief. How could he say such a stupid thing? I was the last person in the world who would be susceptible to depression.

As if he was reading my mind, Dr Haines continued: "Because of your competitiveness, need for achievement and your desire to appear positively to others, I think you often set unrealistic goals for yourself. These unreasonable objectives can be self-defeating when failure to meet perfectionistic standards results in self-blame. Aggravated self-blame can precipitate depression and even a kind of paralysis where you are unable to function adequately or to move forward. You are human, Michael, and humans make mistakes." I sat there amazed. In a single statement, he had captured the essence of my malaise.

Dr Haines asked whether I or anyone in my family had a prior history of depression. When I answered in the negative, he looked at his watch and said: "Based on the fact that you have no prior history of depression and your track record to date, I think your chances of recovery are excellent. But it will not be overnight. I am going to prescribe an antidepressant for you that is also a sedative, but it will probably take at least two weeks for the antidepressant to begin working. Take two before bed at night. It will also help you sleep. For the next few weeks, I want to see you twice a week." We agreed that I would see him every Tuesday and Thursday between 1 p.m. and 2 p.m. I requested lunch time because I still believed I could cope with the depression without Ogilvy & Mather finding out. Then he rose, signalling the end of the session. As we were about to leave his office, he delivered a killer blow by saying: "By the way, I think you should tell your employer about this. But it's your decision."

I left his office feeling old and brittle. I didn't walk so much as shuffle. I couldn't believe the abruptness of my metamorphosis from a single-minded high-flying adman to an angst-ridden mental invalid. I am clinically depressed, I kept repeating to myself in bewilderment. I felt Hilary's hand snuggle into mine, a silent cry for some indication of strength. I looked at her face, drained white by what she had just heard. Her eyes were moist as she smiled wanly at me. There was no hint of condemnation in her voice as she said: "Mike, we'll get through this together. I'll take care of you. Don't worry." Instead of helping me, though, I felt perversely degraded by her words. You're not supposed to take care of me, I thought, it's my job to take care of you. As I watched her dab her eyes with a tissue, I wished I could cry. But I was dry inside. Not once during the next two-and-a-half years would I ever shed a tear.

As we returned home, I thought about the presentation I was scheduled to make the following day. It was an orientation session for a new client that the agency had just won. I had made the presentation many times before, but now the thought of standing up in front of a group of people triggered another panic attack, causing a sharp, almost physical pain. The client and the agency, unaware of my affliction, were expecting my characteristic exhibition of exuberance and energy. That's why they had selected me to showcase the spirit of the agency to new clients.

As I stepped outside to light a cigarette, I began to sweat again. I noticed that my hands were trembling. I saw the dirt underneath my nails and realised I hadn't bathed for three days. I hadn't considered my physical appearance; even the act of showering and shaving seemed beyond me. All I wanted to do was run away. I decided to call the agency to tell them I wouldn't be able to make the presentation. This time when I called my secretary, she didn't have to ask what was wrong. She commented that I sounded terrible. "Don't worry about tomorrow," she said. "After you called this morning, we arranged for someone else to do the presentation. Get better fast, we're already missing you."

I felt a hollow sense of relief. Every act of surrender to the disease made it stronger. But I couldn't fight it. I was convinced that a part of me, the best part, had been amputated. Life had become a horrible place to be. I knew Dr Haines was right. I would have to tell Ogilvy & Mather about my condition. I couldn't disguise the disintegration for much longer.

I began taking the antidepressants that Dr Haines had prescribed. A week passed and then another, then another. But the only effect the drugs had on me was to enhance my lethargy and completely drain my mouth of any saliva. It was difficult enough as it was to summon the strength to face the day. The drugs only made the confrontation with reality every morning that much more excruciating. I discovered very quickly that drugs would not be my salvation. There was no such thing as a "happy pill" that would somehow restore my spirit. I might as well have taken sleeping pills for all the good the drugs did for me. Over the next two-and-a-half years I was to be given a bewildering array of medication. None of it made any impact whatsoever on my condition. For me, the solution lay in a far more drastic measure. But that was still many months and many miles away.

Looking back, I can't believe how much of a crutch my sessions with Dr Haines became. I hung on desperately from session to session. On the days when I was due to see him, I barely made it through the morning, my desire to talk openly with an objective third party was so great. At every session, though, I said exactly the same things and he served up exactly the same platitudes. I complained that the drugs didn't seem to be working and that I thought my condition

43

was getting worse. His response was merely to increase the dosage and tell me to have the patience and perseverance to see it through.

By August, my illness had progressed far enough to produce some of its best-known and most sinister symptoms: confusion, failure of mental focus and lapse of memory. As a consequence, my performance at work deteriorated dramatically. What's more, I believed that my enormous enthusiasm had been the primary force behind my accomplishments. Now that it had evaporated, I became increasingly ineffectual. Clients began commenting to senior management about my lacklustre performance. I became paranoid about the looks I received and the words that were said to me. I felt as if I had mental AIDS. With my ego in tatters, every word penetrated my immune system. I waited for the inevitable call to tell me I was fired. But I still hadn't confided in management about my illness. My last miniscule shred of pride prevented me from doing so. I didn't want sympathy. In a way, I wanted to be punished. I felt I didn't deserve to be part of the company. I didn't even think about the impact of losing my job on my family. Extreme self-centredness and selfishness were two more siblings of depression.

Something happened just before lunch on 22 August that forced me to confess my condition to senior management. I was now chain-smoking. It was the only way I could handle the fear that was gouging me. I failed to put out a match after lighting a cigarette and threw it into the wastepaper basket. The paper in the basket caught alight. Although I smelt something burning, in my anarchical mental state I didn't connect the smell to the basket. All of a sudden I saw the flames. I jumped up and tried to stamp out the fire with my foot, clumsily knocking over the basket in the process. Burning bits of paper scattered all over the floor, singeing the carpet. The smoke drifted into the passageway. Alarmed by the smell, people came running out of their offices. Seeing the smoke, the office manager rushed into my office to witness me crazily trying to extinguish the last remaining burning piece of paper.

Pam Magen, the office manager, was a kindly middle-aged woman who had devoted her life to the company. She was like an aunt to most of the staff, especially the out-of-towners who relied on her to help them acclimatise to their new environment. She was also very close to the chairman. Pam had been especially good to me in my two years at Ogilvy & Mather. I suspected that my rapid rise through the ranks was due in large part to her whispers to the chairman. But now she gaped at me in disbelief. "Michael," she cried, "what is going on here?!" I heard my other voice say involuntarily: "Pam, I'm sick. I'm very sick." Immediately, she turned around and closed the door. Then she sat down on the couch and bade me do the same. In her 25 years with the company, she said, she had seen many stars go through burnout. She told me that over the previous few weeks she had sensed that I was struggling. She had spoken with the chairman and both of them had become increasingly concerned about me.

"I wish it were just burnout, Pam," I said to her, relieved that I didn't have to pretend any more. For the next twenty minutes, I related the events of the previous six months to her, ending with the confession: "Pam, I'm not the same person I used to be. I'm not that good any more. I don't deserve to be here so I'll understand if the company wants me to go." Her eyes filled with compassion. She covered my hand with her own and said: "When we employed you two years ago, we entered into a reciprocal agreement. You would do your best for us and we would do our best for you. For the past two years, you have exceeded all our expectations. You have been very, very good for this company. Now it's our turn. How could you possibly think we would walk away from you when you need us most? Go home now. I'll speak to John [the chairman] and we'll discuss this with you tomorrow." Her decency dumbfounded me. I thought back to when I was a director at Grey Phillips in South Africa. I would never have demonstrated the same care and concern for an employee who was floundering. All I would have seen was a nonperforming overhead that needed to be replaced. I had just been given an awesome lesson in humanity. For a brief moment, it pierced my pessimism. For the time being, I was not destined to be destitute. That night the chairman called me. "Meet me tomorrow at the Prince Edward Hotel on King Street at 8 a.m. for breakfast," he said. "We've got a plan to get you through your difficulties."

The Prince Edward is arguably the most stylish hotel in Toronto. It was also the preferred breakfast venue for the power elite. I had taken many clients there for breakfast, revelling in my role as their strategist and confidant. Now I was there as a casualty, someone who had started the race strongly but collapsed just as the going got rough. I wanted to scream. Instead of blood, it felt as if napalm was running in my veins. I hate you, I said to myself. You don't belong here, you've never belonged here. I slunk into the restaurant, feeling grossly incongruent with the Victorian splendour of the room. Although I was a few minutes early, the chairman had already arrived. He stood up and waved to me.

The chairman was an avuncular man in his early fifties. He was almost completely bald, but with finely crafted features and deep, warm eyes that missed nothing. He shook my hand firmly as we sat down. For about a minute he said nothing, looking at me in a way that conveyed a profound empathy. "Pam told me about your conversation yesterday," he said. "In a way, I think I am partially to blame for the way you feel. I think we gave you too much to handle too soon." I started to remonstrate with him, but he held up his hand and continued. "She also told me of your regret about the house and the large mortgage you are now carrying. So here's our plan for you. We will take over the mortgage on your house. By that I mean Ogilvy & Mather will assume the mortgage from the bank and include your monthly payments as part of your package. As of now, I want you to take four weeks' leave. Spend the first week of your leave with your family at Disneyland. We've booked you and your family into the Holiday Inn in Orlando, Florida and here are four air tickets. When you come back, we'll rearrange your portfolio of accounts. Michael, you have a great future with us. All great men go through a crisis of confidence. This is your rite of passage. I've been there so I know what I'm speaking about. Now relax, don't think about work. Get your strength back. We're with you." With that, he gave me a letter confirming his commitment in writing.

I was overwhelmed by his generosity and belief in me. Shit, I must have been good, I thought, still unable to link my past performance with my current state of mind. But my experience had taken a positive turn. I now began to picture my affliction in heroic terms. I wasn't going through a depression, I was going through a rite of passage. I wasn't heading for the gutter, I was going to be great. The chairman had made me an offer that exceeded my greatest expectations. For the first time in six months, I had good news for Hilary.

Late August is late summer in Canada and I remember 23 August as having as close to perfect weather as Canada gets. It was just past 9 a.m. when I stepped out of the Prince Edward into the early morning sunshine. For once, the humidity level was low and the sun shone warm and nurturing on my face. With nowhere in particular to go, I decided to stroll down to the waterfront, about a kilometre away. When I got there I boarded the ferry to Toronto Island, a strip of land about 500 metres from the mainland. There I spent the next few hours indulging in the rare luxury of being able to think clearly, unpolluted by panic. I ate lunch at one of the many snack bars lining the shore. I never knew that a simple toasted cheese and tomato sandwich could taste that good. My spirit had shifted totally from extreme melancholia to ecstasy. It had been such a long time since I'd known this delicious emotion that it soared into euphoria. This unnatural, wild mood swing should have been a warning to me. I would discover later that it was a manifestation of the particular strain of depression that had infected me. I didn't understand it then, but I was a victim of bipolar depression. This is when the sufferer rocks uncontrollably between extreme emotional highs and lows.

I lay down on a patch of grass in the shade of a maple tree and drifted into a contented sleep. I woke up in the late afternoon. The sun had begun its descent into darkness and the lengthening shadows raked the island. Although it was still warm, I felt slightly chilled. I took out the chairman's letter from my pocket and reread it to make sure it wasn't just a dream. But this time, my elation began to deflate like a punctured balloon. It would be a long time before I would learn my lesson and shed my false ego. Don't kid yourself, it said to me. Things will never be the same for you at Ogilvy & Mather. You're no longer a superstar, now you're just damaged goods. You've lost it. The chairman made you this offer based on how good you were, not on bad you are going to be.

As I boarded the return ferry, packed with holiday-makers enjoying their summer break, I knew one thing with absolute certainty: I was utterly alone in the battle to save my mind. My war was being fought with demons that only I could see, that only I could defeat. I was wrestling with the devil, and back then in the summer of '89, the devil was winning.

5

The Collapse

Something major is about to happen. He's so haunted. Those eyes, they terrify me. Those words coming from his mouth, they shock me. It's awful. I feel powerless – powerless to be responsive, powerless to put my arms around his neck to console him. He repulses me. What's going on? My kids, thank God for them.

HILARY LIPKIN'S DIARY, 5 SEPTEMBER 1989

By the time I returned to the house (I still couldn't think of it as home), all traces of euphoria had gone. In its place, I felt the gloom seeping back into my psyche like rising damp. Despite my melancholia, however, my other self was fascinated by the caprice of my emotions. My moods were like marionettes being jerked around with mad abandon by some out-of-control Mephistopheles. I was becoming mentally incontinent. The one trait that separates man from animal, self-control, was slipping away from me with terrifying speed.

I entered the back yard to a scene of glowing domesticity. Hilary was sitting there with her friends. The children were splashing in the pool, their shrieks of delight bouncing off the water. As Hilary rose to greet me I saw her friends exchange a surreptitious glance. I gave them a perfunctory wave and then went inside. How did it go this morning? Hilary's eyes enquired desperately as she followed me into the house. I took out the letter and gave it to her. As she read it, I could see the wonder and relief sweep over her. "You see," she exclaimed, "we've all got faith in you. This is incredible!" From my other pocket I gave her the plane tickets to Disneyland and told her about the chairman's gesture. She stood there in utter amazement and then threw her arms around me. "We're going to be okay," she whispered in my ear. I remained silent and her resilient naivety took it as consent.

A few days later we boarded the American Airlines 9 a.m. flight to Orlando, Florida, where we were to spend a week at Disneyland. For the children, this was the fulfilment of their ultimate fantasy. Their friends at school had told them all about Disneyland, where Mickey Mouse, Donald Duck and all the other residents of their dreams actually walked around live, shaking people's hands. They had the best daddy in the whole world, they told their friends: he was taking them to where they had always wanted to go.

My son squeezed my hand excitedly as we moved through Orlando airport on our way to the car rental agency. Could we go straight to Disneyland? he asked. He wanted to go on a ride underneath the sea which his friends had told him was "awesome". All around me, little kids were performing the same pantomime with their parents. It was the last official week of summer and the closing week of the long midyear school holidays. Thousands of families from all over the globe were taking this final opportunity to escape from reality before going back to the grind of their everyday existences.

We checked into the Holiday Inn and then drove to Disney's Magic Kingdom, about eight kilometres away. As an adman, I marvelled at the manufacturing of happiness on such a mammoth scale. Every sight, smell and sound was seamlessly sewn together to enchant and entrance the guests. Parents reclaimed their childhood while their children revelled in the tangibility of their dreams. This was a commercialised, Americanised Garden of Eden, a virtual reality screened from fear and worry. But as I walked around, the anxiety mushroomed inside me like some diabolical foetus. I still didn't realise it, but there would be no external salve to my anguish. Even Donald Duck and his friends became creatures sent to taunt and torture me.

My depression was progressing to the next stage of its inexorable development – total passivity. It was a sclerosis of the mind and my emotions were clotting. I couldn't even muster the strength to feel rage and anger any more. I had a sense of helplessness born out of hopelessness. I followed Hilary and the children around the theme park like a zombie.

On our final day in the theme park, the parody of my situation was played out by Mickey Mouse himself. A group of guests had gathered around Mickey Mouse to photograph him with their children, and he obliged with all the affability that has made him the world's favourite character. As we approached the group, Mickey Mouse looked up and saw us. With his rodent intuition, he sensed my distress, left the children clustering around him and walked towards me. To the delight of the group, he mimed my mournful pose and then embraced me, patting me tenderly on the back as he did so. As I heard the click of Hilary's camera, I created a mental snapshot of the absurdity of the moment. There I was, suffering from a disease I was convinced would debilitate me, being consoled by Mickey Mouse to the applause of strangers. I was caught in an outerworld, where nightmare, fear and farce intersect.

Ironically, it was in Disneyland, surrounded by an overabundance of synthetic happiness, when Hilary's belief in me buckled and broke. For seven days, we were together 24 hours a day. As the sun rose each morning and the kids awoke with their magical anticipation of another day of fantasy, I retreated further and further into my shell of mute unresponsiveness. "Jesus, at least pretend to be excited for the sake of the children," she shouted at me one morning.

But all I could do was look back at her uncomprehendingly. At that precise moment, I saw her concern change into contempt. I remember being filled with a sense of morbid achievement. You've finally done it, I thought. You've alienated the one person who refused to give up on you. I had surrendered to my sickness, schizophrenically feeling both relieved and despairing. My mission of self-sabotage was almost complete. I rejected Hilary's belief in me because I couldn't cope with it. I couldn't bear the thought of living up to her expectations so I smashed them. At the same time, I couldn't see my way out of the grave I was lowering myself into. This is what it must be like to be buried alive, I ruminated. I was like a corpse that hadn't died.

As we flew back to Toronto, I knew with an awful certainty that I would never again cope with life. As I sat in the plane, I felt like a hologram. I was there but I wasn't there. I was neither child nor adult. I was not insane yet I was not sane. Part of me was completely lucid, yet I made no sense to anybody, especially to myself. The monstrous maelstrom in my mind was mangling my senses, making me oblivious to everyone else. My only impulse was to run away from the horror haemorrhaging inside me. But where? Where could I run to escape from myself?

The answer came, as it often does, from a totally unexpected source. On the night of our return, like sons in trouble everywhere, I phoned my mother. She was one of South Africa's best-known artists. The themes she explored in her work probed the struggle embroiling me – the battle between faith and despair, between vice and virtue, between pride and humility. She was a deeply religious person, having joined the Hare Krishna movement about two years before. She was also critically ill with cancer. Yet despite her illness, she was deeply concerned about the stories that had been filtering back to her about my behaviour six thousand miles away.

"Mike, what's happening to you?" she asked quietly. After she had heard my story of lament, she said simply: "You don't know it, but you are blessed. This is God's way of telling you to let go of your attachments to irrelevant things. You are not the controller, He is. Listen to Him, Michael, listen to Him. You are on the verge of a breakthrough in your understanding of what life is all about." But all I could think of was that I was on the verge of total collapse. As if she could read my mind, she suggested that I leave Toronto and spend some time with her in Johannesburg where we could talk, think, meditate and pray together. It had been two years since I had last seen her. Before the onset of the depression I was planning to visit her anyway. Johannesburg was about as far away as I could run. I agreed to her suggestion and four days later I was stepping off the plane at Jan Smuts Airport.

As I emerged from customs into the arrivals hall, I saw her standing there, small and delicate. The cancer had begun its terrible work. The vivacious, vibrant woman that I had left two years before now seemed excruciatingly frail and vulnerable. Her mane of fiery red hair was dulled with grey. Her little girl's figure which she had maintained well into her fifties was now close to emaciation. Her face, which had always radiated energy, now expressed the fatigue of her struggle. Yet there was no resignation or self-pity in her bearing. In fact, she seemed empowered by the inner peace that I had come to seek. Her eyes lit up when she saw me, although I could see her shocked surprise at what I had become. I hadn't slept for the past 24 hours. I had hardly eaten. I hadn't bothered to wash or shave on the plane. My physical state mirrored my mental disintegration.

As we embraced, she whispered softly to me: "Welcome home, my son and friend. Just know I am with you all the time, now and forever. Together, we will find you the faith to believe again. You will be guided. Just be patient. It will all come together for you." All of a sudden, I was completely dependent on her for emotional nourishment. I came close to crying then. When I had left her two years before, I felt that I was the master of the universe – the incarnation of success, a role model for all aspiring emigrants to North America.

Now, I had come back broken and defeated. My 31 years had been peeled away to reveal the scared little boy within.

My mother's house was at the corner of Minor and Kenmere roads, at the top of a hill in Yeoville. As we drove past the last remaining blocks to her house, I felt an empathy with the streets that I had never felt in Toronto. Yeoville is probably South Africa's most polyglot suburb. Long before the political liberation of South Africa, Yeoville's potpourri of people had pre-empted change. Nothing could stop the natural flow of people of all shades and persuasions to one of Johannesburg's oldest areas. I think that's why my mother chose to live there. And her house itself was the oldest house in the suburb. Just above the front door, etched in stone, was a date: 1907. She had purchased the house about ten years before and had turned it, literally, into her spiritual home.

As I entered the house I knew I had stepped into another world. The nostalgia of my youth merged with the serenity of my mother's faith. She had applied her extraordinary ingenuity and artistic imagination to transform every aspect of the house into a shrine to the God she had discovered in her time of need. The turn-of-the-century Victorian architecture, constructed from stone, was in stark contrast to the flimsy, soulless house I had left in Toronto. Even the bathroom was captivating, with its old-fashioned bathtub and porcelain-tipped taps. Her paintings and drawings covered the walls, radiating an energy that was almost celestial. I gazed at a drawing she had done of Prabbupada, the founder of the Hare Krishna movement. She had captured him in the middle of a blessing he appeared to be bestowing on all who had the good fortune to look at him. Her depiction of him was so real I could almost feel his presence. The wooden floor creaked as I wandered into my old bedroom. I sat on the bed and looked in wonder at the impossibly high-pressed ceiling with its ornate, flowery design.

I shook my head in disbelief as I thought of the absurd sequence of events over the past few weeks. I had gone from breakfast at the Prince Edward Hotel in Toronto to Disneyland to this place from my past, so far away, both physically and metaphysically, from the world I had chosen to live in. The fact of my life was stranger than any fiction I had ever read. Incredibly, I caught myself smiling. For the moment, the blackness had been pierced. But this mood was not a manic high. I was not filled with the feeling of ecstatic euphoria that overcame me after my meeting with the chairman. Rather, it was a sense of composure. The harmony of my mother's home had temporarily banished my panic. I remember thinking that for the next two weeks I was safe. The bogeyman would not dare enter this place.

I turned to see my mother looking at me. As she stood there framed by the doorway, she looked like someone from one of her paintings. The early morning sun was illuminating her from behind, enveloping her in a kind of halo. I sensed then that she was already on her way to somewhere far beyond my frame of reference. "I've run a bath for you," she said. "Wash yourself and then we'll eat." As I bathed, I felt as though I were engaging in a kind of ritual. I was cleansing both my mind and body.

I walked into the kitchen to find the table laden with fruit, nuts, freshly baked whole-wheat bread and steaming mugs of herbal tea. My mother was sitting there looking out of the window in an almost trancelike state. There was a faint smell of incense in the air and the only sound was the brushing of the leaves from a nearby oak tree against the window. I sat down next to my mother and she squeezed my hand. Despite her illness, I could feel her strength and the callouses on her palm from decades of sculpting and painting. "Let's bless this day and this food," she declared, after which she said grace in the language of her religion. What followed was quite simply the most delicious meal I had eaten in a year.

That afternoon, I went with my mother to the hospital where she was having radiation treatment for her cancer. As we sat in the waiting room together with the other patients and their families, my mother said to me with just a hint of a smile: "There are two ways to look at suffering. You can lament and cry about it, or you can laugh at it and be grateful for the opportunity to stretch your consciousness. But it's not easy. When it actually happens to you it's tough. Mike, this is my greatest challenge. I'm glad you're here to share it with me."

For the next two weeks, the days assumed a sublime pattern. We would awake in the morning just before dawn and pray together. Then we would sit on the porch and talk about what had happened to both of us over the past few years. In the afternoons, a steady stream of visitors, young and old, would come to ask her advice on a myriad of different issues. I realised that she had become a touchstone for an entire community. Although the edge had been taken off my despair, I still hadn't managed to sew together the pieces of my undone mind. My mother had become my emotional dialysis machine. I was feeding off her strength and spirituality. Ironically, her weakened physical state had made her psychologically omnipotent and omniscient. She had tuned into a higher power and her life's mission had become to share it selflessly with all who requested it.

As my departure loomed closer, my apprehension grew stronger. I knew I wasn't ready to confront myself in Toronto again. I fantasised about staying with my mother and even joining the Hare Krishna movement. But I knew I had to go back and endure the trials that lay ahead. If I made one breakthrough in Johannesburg, it was the abandonment of the question: "Why did this have to happen to me?" I knew instinctively that there was some meaning to what I was going through. Over the previous few days, the environment had provided me with the calm to introspect. And while I still didn't like what I saw, I could see the real me at the bottom of the lake. The vision was vague and it was murky, but it was there.

It's 25 September 1989. I am driving to the airport. I am drenched in dread. I am going back to hell. I want to hold on to my mother and hug her and never let her go. Although she's sitting right next to me, she's already fading away. God, I'm frightened. I am not ready to be an adult again. I want someone to take care of me. Where, oh where is my strength? Oh shit, there's the airport. We're slowing down. I'm getting out of the car and handing my luggage to the porter. I'm embracing my mother, maybe for the last time. But she's not crying. She's handing me a note, telling me to read it on the plane. I am walking through customs. Everything is a blur. My mind has fogged up. I am boarding the plane. It's taking off. I unfold the note and read it:

In remembrance of a special time we shared between Toronto and Johannesburg

To my son and friend – Michael Ross

I live in peace and surety

I let go of all fear and doubt of self
I am never limited by past experience or present appearance
I bless and let go of all that serves me no more
I dare to dream anew
I choose what rings true for me
And honour it with love and acceptance

I shed every thought separating me from it
And finally I rest secure in the truth that sets me free
To be all that I can and choose to be.

Your mother – Arca Vigraha Devi Dasi

I still have that piece of paper. In fact, I'm looking at it now as I write this. I've pinned it onto my notice board in my office. It's yellowed and the ink is faded. But every time I read it, I feel that moment with a fresh intensity. Although I would still endure over two more years of agony, my trip to Johannesburg in the spring of '89 saved my sanity by giving me a glimpse of who I could become. It demonstrated that there was something inside me that could ultimately triumph over the demons that had temporarily confiscated my senses. I didn't know how and I didn't know when I would emerge from the morass, but I knew it was not my karma to spend the rest of my life as a depressive.

6

A False Dawn

Job change. Job satisfaction. Love, love, love. The negative energy of the past few months has been replaced by an overwhelming positivity and optimism. The elation I feel for him when he says, "I can't tell you how it feels to be so excited when I wake up in the morning" is wonderful. My God, we're alive. We're through the very worst trauma of our lives. We're united again. But this time we're stronger than before. I have learnt so many lessons. I have learnt patience and what it genuinely means to love someone.
HILARY LIPKIN'S DIARY, 1 DECEMBER 1989

Once again, I found myself emerging from customs into the embrace of family members who loved me. Once again, I saw the look of desperation on Hilary's face. I had been speaking to her from South Africa, telling her that I had found a sense of inner harmony in the company of my mother and that I was hopeful I would be able to function back in Toronto. But as we drove down the highway to our house, my composure melted away.

However, I resolved to go to work three days later. Anything was better than being alone with myself in the house where I would become obsessed about my predicament. I remembered Joseph Conrad's character Kurtz from his classic novel *The Heart of Darkness*. In the novel, Kurtz ventures into the jungle, far from the constraints of civilisation. He goes mad and Conrad describes Kurtz's pain. It's when Kurtz looks inside himself and, in absolute torment, utters the words: "The horror, the horror," at what he sees. Never before had I felt such empathy with another person, fictional or real.

I couldn't tell whether it was my paranoia or my colleagues' newly developed suspicion of me, but when I walked into Ogilvy & Mather after being absent for a month, I sensed that people were involuntarily shying away from me. Looking back, I think it was both. Instead of radiating energy, I was excreting pessimism. I discovered what it was like to be an untouchable. Before the onset of my depression, people would stream into my office throughout the day in the hope that some of my luck would rub off on them. Now, I was in quarantine.

I also came back to a massive shock. In my absence, one of my largest accounts had voiced its dissatisfaction with the agency, partially as a result of my collapse. They had put the account out to "pitch". This meant that Ogilvy & Mather had to "repitch" to retain the account against a number of agencies who had been invited to prove why they should be awarded the business. The presentation was scheduled for the following week. The account was worth R15 million to the agency. It was also part of a much larger group which had placed other business with the agency. If this account walked, it would spark the exodus of even more business. It was an advertising agency's worst nightmare. And I had precipitated it.

The crisis was so severe that the chairman had taken personal control of the repitch. As the person who had managed the account for the previous two years, I was a key member of the team. The situation called for imaginative, bold thinking that would convince the client that Ogilvy & Mather should remain their advertising agency. A repitch, therefore, was an agency's sternest test. They had to overcome the client's dissatisfaction which had caused the repitch in the first place, and still generate enough excitement to prevent the client succumbing to the seduction of a new partner. It was akin to a spouse requesting a divorce and then being wooed back by her husband while divorce proceedings were still being initiated.

It was during the next few days that I lost the faith of the second person who believed in me – the chairman. While he and the rest of the team were rising to the occasion magnificently, I could do no more than mumble trite clichés which served only to raise the team's frustration levels at the most inopportune moments. In the end, I was not even included in the final presentation – another signal to the rest of the company that I was on death row. The final blow was the failure of the company to retain the account. I had become a massive liability. It was one thing for the company to carry a passenger, it was another thing entirely for them to accommodate someone who was sabotaging their business.

The day after the agency was notified that they had lost the account, the chairman called me into his office. This time, I knew there would be no miracle. But my conversation with him exceeded my most dire expectations. While Canadian law prohibited the company from firing me, because I was "officially" sick, the chairman suggested that I consider going back to South Africa because, he implied, I had ruined my reputation beyond redemption in Canada. He advised me that he was also pulling me off all my other accounts immediately for my own good and for the good of the agency.

"Boom" went the first grenade as it exploded inside me. "Boom" went the second and the third. Until that moment I had been living in dreadful anticipation of the words the chairman had just spoken to me. But somehow, I thought I would be rescued before I slipped over the edge. Now, as I hurtled into the void, I was stupefied. I could feel the blood drain from my face. I wanted to stand up and leave his office, but I was convinced that I would faint. The chairman just looked at me. He could see my physical distress but he made no attempt to comfort me. Those days were over. I was greatly overdrawn on the emotional bank account between us. He had no more goodwill to give.

Somehow I staggered out of his office into my own. I locked the door and lay down on the couch. So this is it, I mused as I inhaled deeply on my little stick of nicotine. As I peered at the ceiling through the blue haze of smoke, I thought: this is the end of the Mike Lipkin fireworks display. I had ascended like a rocket, lighting up the sky for one brief moment before ignominiously fading to black. I had absolutely no idea of what to do or where to go next. I had shattered my support systems. I couldn't call Hilary. I couldn't call my mother, having just left her a few weeks before. I had isolated myself from all my friends. So I went into shock. But like an accident victim, the shock anaesthetised me. It flicked the "off" switch on my mental power system and I shut down.

I lay there neither awake nor asleep for about three hours. Then, as the shock wore off, my thoughts began to thrash about like sharks in a feeding frenzy. *I can't go home tonight, I can't tell Hilary what has just happened . . . The shame, the shame I've brought on my family . . . I'm too young to die . . . I know I've got so much potential, but now I'm never going to realise it . . . I can't go back to South Africa as a total failure, it will only get worse there . . . How could things have got so bad so fast? . . . I must be evil to deserve such punishment . . . Maybe Hilary and the kids are better off without me.*

Then it happened, an event so serendipitous that it could only have been orchestrated by a higher power. The phone rang, slicing through my thoughts. At first, I was reluctant to answer it. I thought it must be Hilary, calling as she did every day to find out how I was. She was the last person I wanted to speak to right then. But as I answered the phone, I heard a man's voice. It was Terry Martin, a head-hunter who specialised in the advertising industry. I had met him when I first arrived in Canada and he was impressed with my track record in South Africa. Although I had taken the job at Ogilvy & Mather without his help, he kept me on his radar screen. Over the past two years, he had offered me a few opportunities which I declined. However, my performance prior to the onset of my depression had filtered through to him, making me an increasingly attractive asset to be traded to another advertising agency. *Miraculously, he had no idea of my collapse.* The chairman was wrong, my reputation was not ruined. I had prematurely prophesised my own demise.

"How is it going?" he asked me, ignorant of the irony in the question. For a brief moment I hesitated. If only he knew, I thought. But somehow I kept the chaos out my voice as I responded nonchalantly: "Fine, things are going well for me." "Listen," he said excitedly in his Canadian twang, "I know you've been uninterested in what I've had to offer you in the past. But this time, I've got a once-in-a-lifetime opportunity for you. It's a position made in heaven. You are perfect for it. Don't turn me down on the phone. At least let's discuss it eyeball to eyeball. Trust me on this one. Can we meet tonight? It's urgent." Hope surged through me like an electric current. Instantly, my energy flow reversed from negative to positive. Maybe, just maybe, Terry Martin was throwing me a lifeline. I wanted to meet with him immediately. Although he was ignorant of my situation, I was terrified he would discover the truth in the next few hours through a random conversation with someone who worked with me. However, I knew I couldn't see him that evening. I had been through too much that day. Despite my new-found positiveness, there would be no way I could camouflage my state of mind. Martin was a highly intuitive person who would sense that something was wrong. So we agreed to meet at an out-of-the-way coffee place the following morning. I had the night to psych myself up for the meeting.

As I put the phone down, I pumped the air with my fists and thanked the great adman in the sky. He's still looking after you, I said to myself. Martin's call had reignited my lust for life. Like Lazarus, my belief in myself was raised from the dead. "I can do it, I know I can do it," I chanted to myself. At that instant I was blissfully unaware that this radical mood swing was pathological. All I knew was that it was the sweetest moment of my life. I was going to be saved. I put on my overcoat to leave and as I passed the chairman's office on the way out, I thought: "I'll show you. My best is yet to come. Just watch me."

It was late October. The warmth of summer was already a distant memory as the autumn chill swirled through the streets of Toronto. The bite of the cold seemed to sharpen my feeling of exhilaration. It was as if my blood had been carbonated. My natural effervescence had returned. My entire body tingled with the thought of the new beginning Martin was going to offer me. I raised the collar of my overcoat as I strode purposefully towards the subway. "Please God, let me get this job," I prayed.

I arrived home to the delicious aroma of the roast chicken Hilary was preparing for dinner. I walked into the kitchen and embraced her from behind. I could feel her body stiffen in disbelief. It had been six months since I'd demonstrated such spontaneous affection. I told her about Martin's phone call while omitting to tell her about my traumatic session with the chairman. However, instead of sharing my joy, she asked me: "Are you sure this is what you want? Do you think you can handle it? I don't know if you're strong enough to go into a new job. Don't you think you should speak to Dr Haines about it?" I could see the wariness in her eyes. Her naive optimism had evaporated a long time ago. In its place, there was nothing but fear. She had ceased to see me as her protector. I had become more like her patient.

I looked at her tenderly. My aberrant behaviour over the previous five months had taken its toll on her. Although she had always been very thin, she had lost a lot of weight since the onset of my illness. Her face was pale and drawn from fatigue and worry. The first strands of grey had begun to thread their way through her auburn hair. I realised that I had robbed her of her innocence. I had demolished her utopian existence and plunged her into crisis. Instead of falling apart, however, she had tapped into an inner reserve of strength that kept the family together. I thought of how she continually reassured the children every night that things would be okay while I sat mindlessly watching TV. I thought of the mask of cheerfulness she donned every morning as she went out to work. I thought of the courage she needed to face her friends and the rest of the community with pride, despite her husband's fall from grace. For the first time in five months, I thought of how lucky I was to be with her.

I told her that I needed a change at work. I reassured her that I didn't need to consult Dr Haines on the decision because I knew it was the right thing to do. I said that Ogilvy & Mather wasn't the correct environment for me. It was too big and staid. I needed a more daring company to help me flex my ability. I tried to convince her while trying to convince myself. "I think my job had something to with my depression," I said to Hilary, committing the cardinal mistake of assigning the blame for my state of mind to an external source. "I think I've worked through my problems. I'm ready to face the next challenge. I know I've hurt you and the kids, but I'm going to make it up to you. Trust me," I continued, aware of how much was riding on my meeting the following morning with Terry Martin. For that brief moment I felt the power within me again. And it felt good, really good. My optimism was contagious and I could see Hilary allowing herself to catch it.

I then did something which reinforced the words I had said to her. I polished my shoes. It had been a peculiar ritual of mine ever since I had started working to polish my shoes every night and lay out my clothes for the following day. I took an immense pleasure in looking good. I had read all the literature on power dressing and personal packaging. I knew which colours enhanced my aura of authority and I tailored my attire to the clients I was due to meet the following day. I believed that if you looked the part, it was easier to play the part. And after all, the business of advertising was really show business. I would even discuss my clothes with Hilary before we went to bed. I would ask her advice on whether a particular tie went with a particular shirt. She understood me better than anyone on earth and I would always heed her counsel.

That night, we went to bed and made deep, glorious love, celebrating a tomorrow that once again held so much promise.

I awoke the following morning feeling both excited and terrified. I was about to have the most important meeting of my life. I still didn't know what opportunity Martin was about to offer me, but compared to what I was going through at Ogilvy & Mather, almost anything would be appealing. As I dressed, I saw Hilary watching me. She noticed that my upbeat mood had sustained itself through the night. This was the first morning in five months that I had actually woken up in an enthusiastic frame of mind. That in itself was a positive sign for her. "Wish me luck," I whispered to her as I ran out of the door.

I met Terry Martin at a place called Fran's near his office in Bedford Street in midtown Toronto. I arrived early and rehearsed the meeting in my mind. I would appear calm and interested but not desperate for the job. Martin arrived a few minutes later and made his way to where I was sitting. He was a big man, an ex-professional ice-hockey player whose face still bore the scars of his years in the rink. He was an affable person with a kind of rough-hewn charm. We shook hands and I returned his grip with all the strength that I could muster. "How ya doin', Lipkin?" he bellowed at me. "Great," I grinned with fake sincerity. We indulged in small talk for a few moments and then he put the opportunity on the table.

"Okay, here's the deal," Martin said. "Ambor Kane Livet, AKL, is one of the most creative ad agencies in the city. You agree?" I nodded, holding my breath. AKL were acknowledged as one of the hottest ad agencies in Toronto. They were a medium-sized agency with a reputation for unorthodox but brilliant work. At the advertising award shows every year, they continuously walked away with the lion's share of awards, despite their relatively small size compared to giants like Ogilvy & Mather.

"Well, they have just appointed a new managing director called Richard Kelsy," Martin continued. "Kelsy didn't see eye to eye with their client service director, so the client service director left. They've won a lot of new business recently and they need to replace their client service director urgently. And Mike, I mean *urgently*. I told Kelsy about you. I said that I thought you were born for the job. You're entrepreneurial, you're a maverick, you're creative, your personality will fit AKL's culture like a glove. You've been with Ogilvy for almost two-and-a-half years now. You know the marketplace. Now it's time for you to let loose. Set your talent free, Mike. Talk to these guys. They're hot to trot. And they're willing to pay you big bucks. We're looking at an initial package of C$120 000 (R324 000). On top of that they are offering a share of the profits and the possibility of owning shares in the company. Whaddya say?"

Martin looked at me expectantly. I was astonished. He was offering me a gift from the gods. Even if I had been entirely healthy and happy at Ogilvy & Mather, I would have leapt at this opportunity. "Terry," I said breathlessly, "you've hit the bull's-eye. This is the stuff my dreams are made of. Let's do it." Martin smiled. "I knew you'd like it," he said with satisfaction. "Let's call him now and set up a meeting." He took his cellular phone out of his pocket and called Kelsy. "Hello, Richard," he said, "I'm sitting here with Mike and he's *very* interested in talking to you. When can you meet with him? Tonight?" Martin looked at me. I nodded. "Mike can make it," Martin continued. "You want to meet at your house? Say about 7? Fine, he'll meet you there." As he put his phone away, Martin said to me: "Okay, my friend, this is the big one. Just go wow him and the job's yours. I've done a helluva selling job for you." Martin gave me Kelsy's address and we left.

As we stepped outside, we shook hands and I promised to call Martin the following morning and let him know how the meeting with Kelsy had gone. Although the temperature was near zero, I was flushed. It seemed as if my ordeal of the previous five months was almost over. The fairy tale was about to continue. Luck and serendipity had come to my aid just when I needed them most. But somehow I knew that this fortuitous sequence of events was more than just pure coincidence. Why now? Why, after not speaking to me for almost a year, would Martin call just as I was sliding into the abyss? I was not a religious person then and I am not a religious person now, but I sensed the presence of something extraordinary around me and inside of me. Almost subconsciously, I began to murmur a Jewish prayer of thanks that I had learnt during my years at King David High School in Linksfield, Johannesburg, fifteen years before: *Blessed art thou, O Lord our God, King of the universe, who hast kept us in life, and hast preserved us, and enabled us to reach this season.*

As I returned to Ogilvy & Mather, I realised that I had probably a maximum of two weeks to clinch the deal with AKL before they asked me to leave. Even though they would be forced to give me a "disability" severance package, I knew that I could not allow that to happen. It would be registered on my record and permanently brand me as someone who had suffered a mental illness. I passed Pam Magen's office and our eyes met briefly before she lowered hers. Suddenly, I decided to tell her about the opportunity I was pursuing. I knew she would tell the chairman. At least then they would know I was making plans to leave of my own accord. I thought it might buy me a little more time if I needed it while providing them with some consolation that they wouldn't have to take the painful step of forcing me out.

As I told Pam I saw her expression change from pity to genuine gladness. "That's great, Mike," she said simply. Then, in a moment of remarkable intimacy between two people who hardly knew each other, she told me of her repeated struggle with depression. She told me that she had been to the brink many times. With the help of medication and the support of friends, she had pulled herself back from the edge. I loved her for opening up to me because one of the most pervasive emotions experienced by someone in deep depression is that no-one else on earth has ever experienced such agony. He or she believes that no other human being understands their pain. Although at that moment I believed I had overcome my depression, I still felt its closeness. By sharing her experience with me, Pam let me know that I was not alone and that there were people who empathised with me without judging me.

I spent the rest of the day in the Ogilvy & Mather library researching AKL and their clients. I was determined to impress Kelsy with my knowledge of his ad agency and the work they had done for their clients. As I pored through the magazines and industry journals, my sense of discovery was resuscitated. My mind went into overdrive. I absorbed the information I was studying with a thrilling lucidity. It was as if I had sniffed a mind-enhancing narcotic. I glanced at the clock on the wall. It was almost five o'clock. My date with destiny was fast approaching.

Kelsy lived in the fashionable area of Yorkville, an upscale community of art galleries, expensive shops and some of the best restaurants in the city. I found his house, took a deep breath and rang the bell. Kelsy answered the door. He was in his early forties, a small, slight man whose head somehow seemed too big for the rest of his body. He had birdlike features that reminded me of a sparrow. Even the way he tilted his head and reached out his bony hand to greet me was ornithological. He seemed more cerebral than physical. He invited me into his house which had been decorated tastefully in Art Deco style.

Like me, Kelsy shared a passion for single-malt Scotch. He poured us both a Glenfiddich and we sat down to talk. We soon discovered that we had something else in common: we had both started our advertising careers at Grey Phillips – he in New York, me in Johannesburg. We had a few mutual acquaintances and we discussed their progress for a while. Then he asked me what I knew about AKL, why I wanted to join them and what I thought I could bring to the party. I had just spent the past seven hours preparing for this question, so I launched into a passionate dissertation on the work and philosophy of AKL, how it meshed with my own style and how I thought my expertise could make AKL a better company. When I had finished I could see Kelsy was clearly impressed. A slight smile played about his lips. He looked at his drink and swirled the ice cubes around the glass. "I want you to meet my partners. I'll set up a meeting tomorrow and get Terry to call you," was all he said, but it was enough.

I returned home at about 9.30 p.m., still intoxicated by my meeting with Kelsy. Hilary saw me beaming and said: "I take it the meeting went well." "Unbelievable," I replied as I told her all about it. I had now been "up" for almost two days, and my positive frame of mind seemed to be getting stronger all the time. "I thought I'd lost you but you've come back to me," she said with delight. "I just hope it lasts," she added with an intuitive sense of what was still to come.

The call from Terry Martin came through just after ten o'clock the following morning. He confirmed what I already knew. Kelsy wanted me. "I don't know what you said to the guy, but you blew his socks off!" Martin shouted into the phone. "Can you meet the other guys on Friday evening after work?" I groaned inwardly. Friday was still two days away, a full 48 hours. I wanted to seal the deal immediately. It was a miracle that Martin hadn't yet heard anything about my collapse. Anything could happen between now and then. I felt an immediate spasm of anxiety. But I merely voiced my assent.

Somehow I gritted it out over the next two days. It helped that my love of reading had returned. With nothing to do at work, I spent hours browsing among the plethora of bookstores in downtown Toronto. I had one favourite store called Leichtmanns on Yonge Street. It was a small place but it was packed from floor to ceiling with books on every imaginable subject. The proprietor was an old man with kind eyes who wore his reading glasses on his nose even when he wasn't reading. We had struck up one of those relationships that don't require conversations, just a mutual love of something wonderful – in this case, books. I remember thinking that one day I wanted to write a book that would have its own place on those hallowed shelves.

Every time I returned to the office, I expected to see a message from Terry Martin enquiring about some disturbing news he had just heard about me. Every time the phone rang I expected to hear his voice calling off the meeting. But he never called and eventually Friday evening rolled around.

Ambor Kane Livet's offices were in a recently converted warehouse on Eglinton Avenue in midtown Toronto. My meeting with Kelsy's partners was set for 6 p.m. but I arrived a few minutes early. The layout of the agency was open-plan, with one huge room painted in pastel colours – light blues, greens and pinks. The ceiling must have been forty feet high. Naked air ducts ran along the entire length of the room which took up a complete block, and the whole street-facing side was sheer glass. The net effect was breathtaking. It seemed the antithesis of Ogilvy & Mather – relaxed, informal, intimate. My pulse started to race with desire. I paced up and down with a mental hard-on. I knew Ambor Kane Livet was the right job at the right time for me.

Kelsy came through to the reception at just after 6 p.m. His obvious excitement mirrored my own. He took me through to the area designated as the boardroom where his partners were sitting having a drink. As we entered, Kelsy introduced me, saying: "Guys, I'd like to introduce you to Mike Lipkin, a person who has impressed me more than any other client service person I've met in this city. Mike is excited at the opportunity we may have for him and I'm excited at the prospect of having him join us." I smiled to myself at Kelsy's tactics. Right up front, he had given me his unambiguous endorsement. I realised then that this meeting was merely a formality demanded by protocol. It was Kelsy's call, and the decision to hire me had already been taken.

It transpired that one of the partners, Gary Kane, had a couple of close friends who were ex-South Africans. This was not surprising in a city where close to 50 000 South Africans had made their home. But Kane gave me a further vote of confidence by saying that he thought South Africans were an extremely focused and industrious tribe of people. We spoke for another hour or so. And the more we spoke, the more apparent it became that I had established a superb rapport with all of them.

Eventually, Kane and Livet left, leaving Kelsy, Ambor and myself. Ambor was the chairman of the company and the financial director. From the leather folder lying in front of him, Ambor drew out a piece of paper. It was a formal job offer containing the terms Terry Martin had already discussed with me. I read it through slowly, feeling the elation beginning to dance within me. "So what do you say?" Kelsy asked, pushing me for an immediate decision. I wanted to scream "Yes! Yes! Yes!" but I managed to rein in my emotions. Instead, with a voice that didn't seem to belong to me, I responded coolly: "Let me discuss it with my wife over the weekend and I'll get back to you on Monday morning."

For the second time in less than three months, I presented Hilary with a fabulous career offer from the chairman of a highly successful company. But this time it was she who was silent while I erupted in celebration. I had hurt her too deeply too many times for her to suddenly embrace my elation. "If this is what you want, I'll support you," she said in a neutral voice.

It's Monday 22 October 1989. I'm calling Richard Kelsy to accept the job at AKL. My hand is trembling as I hold the phone. Kelsy answers. I tell him my decision. I also tell him that the moment I tell Ogilvy & Mather, they will request me to leave immediately. He expresses his delight. We agree that I will start work at AKL next Monday. I put the phone down, saturated with relief. I've made it. I've fought the demons and won.

But the demons had merely been caged, not killed. Within two months I would free them to continue wreaking their havoc with my mind.

7

Point of No Return

I thought 1990 was going to be our year. Well maybe I ought to clarify that to "my year". It seems as though Michael has chosen to suffer again. The thrill of the job change soured after a few months. His enthusiasm for the opportunity was electric. He said it was unquestionably the "right one". Who would have thought he would allow himself to retreat again into this moronic, idiotic state. It's like a comedy at play – so ridiculously negative and self-tormenting.

The poisonous smell of smoke emanates from his nostrils, from his already nicotine-stained teeth and fingers. Coupled with the nervous sweat spilling from every pore in his body, it yields an odour that scares my very soul. What happened to the romance, the sweet smell of roses and the silver spoon?

We sold the Coral Harbour house and now we're living in the loveliest semidetached house on Charnwood Crescent. I will not allow him to destroy me. I will pull myself out even if I have to do it alone – it will not be my choice but his. My kids will survive and so will I. I will live to make them well adjusted and happy. They will love Michael for who he is – not for who he wants to be or what he was.

The frightening part of this whole experience for me is the shock of this ideal opportunity he spoke about turning into a "sentence". All his problems were sorted out. We sold the house. We reduced the size of the mortgage that was worrying him. He got the job he was looking for. Trustingly, I thought he had made a good decision when he decided to move. His life could be perfect but he is determined to screw up everything God gives him. He's going to lose it all, including us.

My children are just beautiful. I'm embarrassed that they have to witness their father's behaviour and my anger with him. I try to be honest with them. I think they intuitively realise the stresses dad is going through which implicates mom and that's breaking my heart. But they still love their daddy very much. I know Mike can be a good father if only he would let himself.

I love Carla and Anthony more than I can verbalise. When I look at them, I can't believe they're mine. My twins are almost six years old. Carla is athletic and a beautiful dancer and so, so charming. Anthony is less athletic but so caring and loving. He tends to display his emotion by losing his temper. I'm worried about that. Carla is also crying too much for a little girl who's only six years old. I thought we had been through the worst but it seems like it's only just beginning.

I know it's probably an impossible dream, but all I want is to settle down so that we can perhaps have another child. I would love that.

HILARY LIPKIN'S DIARY, 2 JUNE 1990

I started work at AKL on Monday 29 October 1989. Besides being responsible for the client service group, I was also put in charge of some of the agency's most important accounts including Honda and Harvey's, the second biggest fast-food chain in Canada. I was branded as the "hotshot from the big shop" (Ogilvy & Mather). Kelsy had sung my praises and Kelsy himself was one of the most highly regarded admen in Canada. If he said I was good, the rest of AKL reasoned I *must* be good.

The week after I started work at AKL, I had my last session with Dr Haines. I told him about my job change. I said that I had regained my mental health and that I didn't require his services anymore. "Michael," he said gently, "I don't think that's a good idea. Your convalescence is still very delicate. I'm glad you've recovered so dramatically but that in itself is a dangerous sign. It could be just another symptom of the radical mood swings you've been experiencing. It can take months for people to really get over the severity of the kind of depression you've been through since you first saw me in July. I would advise you strongly not to end our sessions." But I hadn't yet learnt to listen. In my euphoric state, I was convinced that my need for therapy was over. Once again, it was a deafness that would cost me dearly.

In the next two months, I did the best work I had ever done. Like an aspirant actor who wins the lead role in a Broadway play, I stretched myself beyond myself. My inspiration was drawn from the huge reservoir of gratitude I felt towards the company for having given me a second chance. I really loved the people who worked with me – both the agency staff and my clients. They sensed this affection and returned it in kind. My enthusiasm and energy levels soared to almost superhuman heights. I was deliciously empowered, continually originating breakthrough ideas that captivated the people around me. Once more, I was living the dream and my God, it felt wonderful!

This halcyon period climaxed on the night of 15 December at AKL's annual Christmas party held at a French-Canadian restaurant called Montreal Bistro in downtown Toronto. It was one of those exquisite winter evenings. The temperature was around zero but there was no wind. The snow was falling down gently, like icing sugar being sprinkled on a cake. I remember thinking during the twenty-minute cab ride to the restaurant that life couldn't get much better than this. My fellow passenger, a young account executive who reported to me, was eagerly telling me about the assignments she had succesfully completed that day. I looked at her and smiled. Her name was Sarah Rowan, an intelligent, attractive girl who was one of the agency's rising stars. "That's excellent, Sarah. Keep it up," I responded, seing the warm glow of recognition light up her face. I felt proud of myself. I had pulled myself out of the quagmire, I was nurturing the people around me, I was trying to be the best I could be.

Like company Christmas parties all over the world, that evening was dedicated to riotous partying. AKL had had a lucrative 1989 and the next year looked even better. In his address to the agency, Kelsy spent a couple of minutes celebrating the fact that I had joined the agency, highlighting my performance during my brief stay with the company. The audience applauded wildly. That night, my shares were at an all-time high.

At around midnight, Don Ambor, the chairman, approached me and put his arm around me. He was in his mid-fifties, a trim, fit man with a shock of white hair and a chiselled face etched with the lines of a life lived to the full. Ambor grew up penniless. With no money to go to college, he started his career as an apprentice printer. By the time he was thirty, he owned his own printing company. That's when he met Gary Kane and Peter Livet, both successful admen at the time. Ambor decided that advertising was more fun than printing and the three of them started Ambor Kane Livet. It was well known, however, that Ambor had made himself a lot of money. After 25 years, he wanted to get out of the business.

"Hey, Mike, I hope you're having a good time," he said to me, slurring his words slightly. I nodded, pleasantly inebriated myself. "One day, Mike," he said, waving his hand at the people around us, "you'll own this agency. I'm getting too old and so are Gary and Peter. It's time to hand this place over to young guys like you and Richard. You've made a big difference to this agency already and so Richard and I have agreed to give you a Christmas bonus equal to one month's salary even though you've only been with us for two months. By this time next year, I'll make you a partner if you continue to perform the way you've been doing." I raised my glass of Scotch to him. "Cheers, Don," I said, filled with a sense of camaraderie. "You're a scholar and a gentleman and I'm proud to work *for* you right now. If I can do as good a job as you've done I'll do very well. Thanks for the gift, it's a great gesture and I really appreciate it."

Ambor had served me my future on a platter. The only way to make real money in advertising was to own a stake in an agency and reap the profits. In just twelve months' time, I would have achieved this objective, but it *was* too good to be true. It would take me another three years to understand it, but deep in the bowels of my psyche I didn't feel as though I deserved to succeed. My pride and self-respect were still built on sand. I had not yet knitted together my fragmented personality. And my flawed value system would continue to sabotage me.

With the bonus that Ambor had paid me, I took Hilary and the kids to Vancouver over the Christmas break. This time we were going away with joy in our hearts, not running away out of desperation. Vancouver is a beautiful city which bears a striking resemblance to Cape Town – the same laid-back feeling, the mountains which carve themselves majestically into the ocean and a mild, if somewhat wet, climate. We stayed at the Inter-Continental, a five-star hotel overlooking the Pacific. My wanderlust had returned and my son and I left Hilary and Carla at the hotel for a day and drove down to Seattle, another favourite city of mine, about 200 km south of Vancouver. It was a glorious vacation. It was also the last holiday we would take together as a family for almost three years.

Something happened to me during the vacation. It was as if the magic spell had been broken. I arrived back at work on 2 January with a vague feeling of uneasiness. At first, it didn't affect my performance at all. In fact, for the rest of January and February I proceeded at a turbo-charged pace. It was as if I was trying to outrun the bogeyman whose sinister presence had re-established itself in the penumbra of my mind.

It was during this time that I met Max Levy, one of Toronto's best-known psychiatrists. AKL retained Max as a consultant on the emotional nuances to be woven into their advertising. I would meet with Max frequently, but as a colleague, not a patient. He was a gentle man in his early fifties, completely bald except for a few tufts of white hair fringing his dome. He had an uncanny insight into the nature of human desire and how to exploit it. In fact, many of AKL's most effective advertising campaigns were the result of his counsel. The two of us generated an instant personal chemistry, but every now and then I caught him looking at me strangely, as if he had seen something that disturbed him but which he didn't understand. Within three months, his instincts would be validated. For almost a year, I would be one of his most problematic patients.

By March, my feeling of uneasiness abruptly became overwhelming. Ecstasy metamorphosised into agony with a devastating suddenness. But it wasn't the acute panic which had assaulted me that first night in June 1989. It was an undulating fear that flowed through me now, rising and falling on its own volition. It wasn't just a mental anguish; the pain was acutely physical. Every time it surged, I felt my insides being ruptured. I would be sitting in my office, conducting a meeting or merely walking around, when I would almost double over with fear. It would come from nowhere, pulled by a current that mocked my puny resistance. I realise now that what had started as a reactive depression, sparked by my reaction to the purchase of the house, had now become endogenous depression – depression fuelled from within, the result of a diseased mind and body looking at the world through twisted lenses.

We even managed to sell the house and move into a smaller semidetached place up the road. My mortgage was reduced drastically, but it made no difference to my spirit. As Dr Haines said it would, the fear burst through the thin wall of confidence I had constructed over the previous few months. The doubt flooded back, sweeping away my self-affection and my affection for the people around me. My discomfort with myself translated itself into a discomfort with others. My courage had collapsed and with it, my ability to lead. The day-to-day problems which are part of any service business became insurmountable difficulties. Instead of supporting my staff, I castigated them for making mistakes. I became intolerant of others' opinions, dictating to them instead of relating to them. And worst of all, I became envious and resentful of Richard Kelsy. I questioned his judgement, I challenged his authority, I undermined his stewardship of the agency. My gratitude towards AKL for saving my career had evaporated, its place usurped by a perverse discontent. And with the discontent came a restlessness. After only five months, I decided it was time to move again.

I blamed everyone around me for the increasing antagonism which was inflaming my relationship with my colleagues. Every glare, every disagreement, every argument reinforced my belief that the people around me didn't understand or appreciate me. "I was wrong about AKL, they're too small for me. I am suffocating here. They can't share my vision. I really belong in a big international agency," were my grandiose thoughts. I had just escaped from Ogilvy & Mather, but in my confusion I now wanted to imprison myself in another multinational company. Looking back, I believe I had become addicted to crisis. Whenever something good and wholesome was placed in front of me, my first impulse was to destroy it. Like an addict shooting up an overdose, I was about to go beyond the point of no return.

One of the people I had met during my initial interviewing process back in 1987 was a man called David Kingsley. He was now the managing director of a large multinational advertising agency called BBDG. He lived around the corner from us and his kids went to the same school as mine. We would bump into each other occasionally. Every time we met, he would let me know that BBDG were interested in talking to me. So now I called him. "Let's talk," I said, taking my first step towards the final demise of my career in Canada.

Kingsley responded warmly, letting me know that there was a "major opportunity" at BBDG. I felt the fatal rush of excitement, yet another horrible hoax being played on me by my depression. I had become a cardboard cutout of a human being, incapable of handling the real dramas that were part of real life. So I hoodwinked myself into thinking that it would always be easier and more exciting on the other side. Unwittingly, I had discovered a timeless fact – if you run away from life too many times, eventually you become powerless to confront it.

I met Kingsley in the middle of April 1990. BBDG had the Chrysler car business, the largest account in the agency. They needed a seasoned professional with "international" experience to manage it. My experience in South Africa and its reputation as a world-class centre of advertising endowed me with a "global" profile. Once more, I found myself being interviewed by a series of executives scrutinising my potential value to their company. But I was a genius at the interview process. After all, it was merely a mutant expression of my neurotic self-obsession. Once more, I dazzled them with charisma. How were they to know it was charisma without a particle of substance?

On 3 May 1990, BBDG offered me the position of senior vice president in charge of the Chrysler account. But this time I perused the offer with shock and not with exultation. I had courted BBDG with a myopia bordering on blindness. I had chased the spurious thrill of flattery and acclaim without even thinking whether I really wanted the job. I was making life-changing, life-shattering "indecisions" based on my prevailing emotions without any consideration of their consequences. Intuitively I knew that going to BBDG was the worst move I could make. But depression had placed a stone wall between me and my intuition. I had become so used to lying to myself that I was unable to tell the truth. I believe now that the genesis of my depression, and the fuel which sustained it, was my constant refusal to heed the advice the voice within us all gives us. The word "intuition" comes from the Latin term *intuare* which means teacher. But the teacher only appears when the student is ready. And I still had a long, tortuous odyssey ahead of me.

While I was writing this chapter, a friend of mine said that he wondered how I could revisit such poignant experiences without encouraging their recurrence. I replied that while I could remember each minute of my three-year struggle in graphic detail, I remember the experiences as belonging to someone else. The decisions I made over and over again were so screwed up that even now I find myself shaking my head. But that's what depression does. It butchers reason. It dismembers its victim's perception of reality into long thin strips of macabre thoughts and impulses. And that's where I found myself that evening of 3 May 1990, hanging between the certain knowledge of personal Armageddon if I went to BBDG and my phobia of slow asphyxiation at AKL.

I had inextricably bound my identity and sense of fulfilment to my job and other people's perceptions of my worth. I had placed my self-esteem in the hands of others. My sense of wellbeing pivoted entirely around my work. My family was a distant concern, subservient to the opinions of near strangers and mild acquaintances. This was the imbalance that would prove almost terminal.

"What the hell do you want me to say?" Hilary screamed at me in anger and incredulity. "For the past month, all you've talked about is BBDG. You said that it was all you wanted. Now you tell me that you don't know what to do. I can't take you any more, Michael. I can't live your life for you. And I don't know how much longer I can live with you. You're driving me crazy." I cringed from her as if her words were physically hitting me. I had promised to call Kingsley with a decision that evening. It was already past 9 p.m. I had to call him in the next few minutes. It wasn't too late. I could still turn BBDG down. I felt the urge to be sick again. After four weeks of interviews and negotiation with both BBDG and Chrysler, it just didn't make sense to turn them down, especially after I had initiated the contact. But after only six months at AKL, it didn't make sense to leave. Like a rabbit on a freeway frozen in the headlights of an oncoming vehicle, I had set myself up for annihilation.

Severe depression is a mental implosion, an absolute collapse of faculties and reason on top of each other. And so the ability to make a decision was buried in the dust and rubble of my mind. I couldn't call Kingsley to say "yes" and I couldn't call him to say "no". So I did nothing. I just paced up and down the passageway, frenetically lighting up one cigarette after another. "I don't know what to do, Hilary. I just don't know what to do," I wailed. But she shot back at me with venom: "You can't behave like this, Michael. You can't treat people this way. You're supposed to be a professional." Coughing from the smoke of my cigarettes, she yelled: "You're going to lose both jobs. This is madness. You've got it all and you want to throw it all away. Well, I'm telling you, if you screw this up again, I'm leaving you. It's been almost a year now, a year of utter insanity and it's getting worse. I've tried to understand you, I've tried to support you, I've tried to help you. But you don't seem to care a damn about me and the kids. All you care about is your stupid job and you can't even get that right. Maybe you need the shock of losing your family. Let's see how you do on your own."

I was immobilised. My thoughts were turning over in my head like clothes in a washing machine. Every word Hilary spoke merely accelerated the cycle. I put the back of my hand in my mouth and bit hard, as if the pain would somehow stop the churning. But the more I ruminated, the more impossible it became to call Kingsley. At that moment, I didn't even know what I would say to him. I couldn't bring myself to commit myself to a course of action I knew would be catastrophic. Yet I didn't have the courage to turn him down. When you can't face yourself, you can't face anybody else. It was now past 10 p.m., too late to phone Kingsley. "I'll call him in the morning. I've still got the whole night to think about it," I deceived myself, procrastination being the last refuge of depression.

By 11 p.m., Hilary had gone to sleep, exhausted and exasperated by my behaviour. But sleep was the furthest thing from my mind. I sat in the dark, the only light coming from the glow of the TV screen and my ever-present cigarette. Time moves very slowly for a depressive. When tomorrow is the worst day of your life, you stretch the now. I reckoned I had to call Kingsley by 8 a.m. the following morning. That gave me nine hours to decide, an eternity for residents of depression. Every now and then I glanced at my wristwatch. Each passing minute heightened my sense of foreboding. I must have dozed off at around 3 a.m. because the last thing I remembered was the rolling titles of some B-grade film.

I awoke to the sound of Hilary packing the kids off to school. It was 7 a.m. I was still no nearer making the call to Kingsley. In the end I didn't have to because he called me fifteen minutes later. "Good morning, Mike," he said in a relaxed, friendly voice, "I'm sorry for calling you first thing in the morning but I was expecting your call last night. I'm on my way to a meeting with the client who's very excited about the fact that you are joining us. I promised him I would confirm your appointment this morning. Can I?" Kingsley had chosen his words cunningly, positioning this conversation as a mere confirmation of a decision that had already been taken. At the same time, he carefully stroked my ego. "Yes," I said simply, letting Kingsley make the decision for me. The die was cast.

There are many ways to commit suicide. You can obliterate yourself immediately with a bullet; you can drift into permanent sleep through an overdose; or you can commit suicide by instalments, which is what I was doing. When every waking moment is lived in despair, despair becomes a state of mind. It also becomes seductive. I capitulated because it was far easier to yield to its gravitional pull than fight it. That took courage, but I was filled with cowardice. I had abdicated my fate to the dark side.

I drove to AKL that morning as though I was driving to a funeral – my funeral. I'm going to miss you guys, I thought melancholically as I entered the agency for the last time. I walked into Kelsy's office and closed the door. He was poring over a major presentation he was due to give that afternoon. He looked at me enquiringly. "Richard, I'm resigning from AKL," I said in a leaden voice. "I've been offered a vice presidency at BBDG and I've decided to accept it." Kelsy's eyes opened wide in astonishment. "Are you mad?" he asked me incredulously after taking a few moments to register what I'd just said to him. "You're leaving AKL for them? They're in deep shit, you know." I didn't know. His words pumped into me like bullets. He stared at me in contempt. "If you want to go to BBDG, you never belonged at AKL. There's something wrong with you, Michael," he spat with rising fury. "Pack up your things and leave."

I drove home very slowly, choking on the regret and remorse I knew I'd feel but was powerless to prevent. It's a terrible thing to give up on life, but that's what I had done. I felt like a useless pariah to myself and everyone around me. I was exhausted from the futile struggle I'd ensnared myself in for almost a year. All I wanted to do was sleep. If only I could stop the tape of my life, I thought, but the torment stretched out endlessly in front of me.

I arrived home at about 11 a.m. The children were at school and Hilary was working. Only the dog was at home and even she cowered away from me as if she could smell my despondency. I went into the bathroom and took a sleeping pill. Then, without even taking off my suit, I went into the bedroom, closed the door, drew the curtains and lay down on the bed.

At about 4.30 p.m., Hilary woke me up. Terry Martin was on the line. Kelsy had called him to tell him the news. Martin was embarrassed as well as financially prejudiced by my action. He had been responsible for selling me into AKL, and his contract with them mandated a refund of a large part of his commission if I left within six months. Furthermore, I had greatly eroded his credibility with the company. They would doubt his judgement in his future dealings with them.

But unlike Kelsy, Martin wasn't angry. I discovered later that after he had placed me with AKL, he had found out about my collapse at Ogilvy & Mather. With the second chance he had offered me at AKL, he hoped it wouldn't recur. When it did, he was disappointed but not totally surprised. "Hey, Mike, are you all right?" he asked with the kind of compassion one reserves for the seriously ill. He reiterated Kelsy's comment about the corporate health of BBDG and then suggested softly: "Maybe you should get some help. But I think you've really set yourself up for failure this time. I hope, though, that things go okay for you." With that he put the phone down. I never saw or spoke to him again. Another ally had been lost. I had become a master at losing friends and alienating people.

I heeded Martin's advice. The next day I got help by calling Max Levy. He hadn't heard that I'd left AKL so when he answered the phone he naturally assumed that I was calling him about a business issue. "Max, I'm in trouble," I said, "I think I've made a terrible mistake. I need your help." I told him about my depression and my decision to join BBDG. I heard him heave a deep sigh. "Michael, I thought I sensed something wasn't right. It's a great pity you didn't speak to me before." he said empathetically. "I would never have let you leave AKL. But what's done is done. If you put yourself in my hands, I'll get you through this. Trust me." I had to trust him. I had no choice. I was being swept away by my torrent of fear and Max Levy was the only thing I had to hold onto.

8

Hospitalisation

Max has become Mike's new psychiatrist. Who would have believed we would find ourselves in such a crisis again? We've reached the point where I've asked Michael to move out. He is staying at his cousin's for a while for the kids' sake. How can they believe in our love if all they witness is hysteria? I wish in my heart that Michael would get on with the job at BBDG, but I fear and dread what we might still face – the loss of that job and the possibility that Mike may find himself with nothing.

It's so exhausting. I'm trying so hard to be strong, controlled and sane but inside I'm just breaking. I'm lonely and scared but I love him. He's a hard guy to give up on. I've seen first-hand how good he can be. I just wish he'd see the light and get going at BBDG. He's got to keep his job at all costs. The alternatives are so unknown, so scary.

I have just reread my diary of when the kids were babies and I feel so sad. So sad that so much time has passed and we're still going through so much pain. All I wish is for Mike's restored faith in himself and maybe one day to feel the joy of being a mother again.

I don't feel well tonight. I had a hernia operation four weeks ago and I feel like I'm cramping up. I'm pushing myself too hard. I'm trying so hard to feel a positive mental attitude that I forget about the surgery. I wish Mike would help me through this but he's not even here.

HILARY LIPKIN'S DIARY, 12 JULY 1990

Mike is home and he's different. Things could be chan-
ging.

HILARY LIPKIN'S DIARY, 5 AUGUST 1990

I was wrong. I'm let down again. It's not going to work.
Why? This is worse than I feared. I am so numb by his
behaviour, so sick in the stomach, so nauseatingly sad. I
think we're going to have to separate, but on a more
permanent basis.

I feel like going home to mom and dad. I feel like
running away from all this and never returning. Maybe I
don't but our kids deserve more. I cannot give them a
decent life here with Mike. It's so unfair for them.

I leave for Calgary tomorrow to celebrate a birthday
with my sister Margot. But I go with such a heavy heart
and no hope. Just fuck Michael. Why do I love him? What
is it about him that makes me love him?

HILARY LIPKIN'S DIARY, 12 AUGUST 1990

Can you believe it's now the 22nd of September? Every-
thing I see is black. I have to get through this for Carla
and Anthony. It's so sickening and frightening. This man
is behaving like scum, the scum of the darkest earth. I
witness behaviour that makes me cry from disgust and
pity. But I hate to pity him. He's so passive, so out of
control. Dear God, what will happen? Save me please,
save me and my kids.

HILARY LIPKIN'S DIARY, 22 SEPTEMBER 1990

What has unfolded since my last entry last year is just
unimaginable. Mike was forced to resign from BBDG last
October. Since then it's been a downhill battle. There are
times when I feel like saying to him just fuck you. I'm
getting out of this relationship. It's probably easier to go
through with divorce, or is it? I still don't know what
keeps us together.

To continue with events. I went to South Africa for a
month and left Michael alone in the house. Well, he just
went over the edge. He's now in hospital – to be exact, he's

87

in the psychiatric ward at the North York Hospital about fifteen kilometres from here. He is severely depressed and the symptoms that go with his illness are too sickening to write about. He's been there for two weeks so far and he probably still has a month to go. He's on intensive anti-depressant drug therapy and hopefully this will bring his behaviour more under control. It's almost as though I'm scared of him, not because of what he'll do to me but what he'll do to himself. He just wants to hurt himself all the time.

If he ever gets out of hospital he's got an enormous battle ahead of him. Not only does he have to get his career back on track, he's got to come to terms with himself. Do I want to be a part of this? I'm not sure. I feel like I'm living through some kind of script and as the weeks go by so the plot unfolds. Will there be a happy ending? At this stage I'm not sure.

Max is no longer Mike's psychiatrist. I think Mike almost drove him crazy. So now he's washed his hands of us. I can't speak to him any more. I need to find someone to speak to because I'm living on the edge of my nerves and my feelings of fear and confusion are intense.

The kids are witnessing something that only happens to others. It's so hard on them. I don't know if they'll ever again experience those thrills we had three years ago. They're growing up so fast. Carla has lost three teeth and Anthony got his first love letter – he's gorgeous. But as far they're concerned, I'm the bad one. They keep asking me why I shout at dad all the time. It's just awful.

HILARY LIPKIN'S DIARY, 27 JANUARY 1991

12 May 1990, the Saturday night before the Monday I was due to start working at BBDG. The senior directors of BBDG threw a party at an upscale French restaurant in downtown Toronto to welcome me into the corporate fold. It was a grotesque climax to the most horrific day of the entire eleven-month ordeal.

I remember waking up that morning with a corrosive loathing of life and self. I wasn't certain whether the burning in my chest was real or hallucinatory. But I didn't care. I would have welcomed a coronary as the easy way out. The brutal fact was that I had lost faith in myself. I couldn't trust myself any more. I couldn't trust what I thought, what I said, what I did. I knew with a schizophrenic insight that I was drawn to destructive decisions the way insects are drawn to the flame that devours them. And so I lay in bed until just before three o'clock, indulgently fantasising about how I could terminate my ugly existence.

"For God's sake, it's almost three o'clock" Hilary shouted at me as she burst into the bedroom, ripping open the curtains and tearing the duvet off me, leaving me lying naked on the bed. "Get up, Goddamn you, get up!" she yelled as she tried to pull me off the bed. As I lay there, with my torso arched and my head almost on the floor, I just stared vacantly at her in mute silence. She kicked me hard in the stomach. Still I said nothing. I felt incapable of responding. She knelt down and hit me across the face with the back of her left hand, her wedding ring catching me on the cheek just under my right eye. "Oh, Michael," she half begged, half screamed, "Show me that you're still alive. Fight back, shout back. Do anything but don't be such a passive slug."

"Stop it, please stop it," a terrified and tearful six-year-old voice cried. My son had run upstairs into the room to be confronted with the scene of his mother screaming at his father lying naked on the floor with a trickle of blood running down his face. He ran towards me and embraced me. "Leave him alone, Mom!" he shouted at Hilary, "Dad's done nothing wrong." Hilary began to cry convulsively and fled the room. As I sat there holding Anthony's trembling little body, I realised that we had become a severely dysfunctional family. Our life was progressing like the screenplay of a badly written made-for-TV movie. And yet through it all, my son's love and faith in me remained profound and unshakeable. "It'll be okay, it'll be okay," I whispered to him without conviction, not knowing how and not knowing when.

I put on some clothes and went downstairs. Hilary was

sitting outside in an awkward position. Her head was almost between her knees and she was pressing both her hands against her lower abdomen. "What's wrong?" I asked her as I went outside. But she just looked at me with a terrible sadness. Her actions of a few moments earlier had shocked her. The blood had completely drained from her face. Her eyes, it seemed, had turned to stone. We both knew that she was desperately trying to resist the undertow of my depression. At that moment, though, she was failing. My relentless gloom was destroying her spirit and wearing out her physical reserves. An old hernia problem had begun to plague her again. She hadn't told me, but she had booked herself into a local hospital to undergo surgery the following month.

As I lit a cigarette she said to me emotionlessly: "You are going to have to leave. You are destroying this family and I will not allow it to continue." I sucked a little harder on my nicotine pacifier. Leave? I thought, where would I go? As if she were reading my thoughts, Hilary said to me: "I have already spoken to your cousin. Dalya says you can stay in her basement for the time being. But you've got to get out of here." Dalya Malkow was my first cousin who lived about a kilometre away with her husband and four children. Moving into her basement would be the ultimate embarrassment. It would have required very little effort to rent an apartment, but even that required too much energy for my depressed mind to muster.

It was on that note that we drove downtown to our rendezvous with the directors of BBDG, incongruously to celebrate the start of my new "career" with them. I found a parking place a few blocks away from the restaurant, a place called Centro's which was a favourite amongst the Toronto advertising community. I glanced at Hilary as we walked an estranged few metres apart. She was scared and bewildered. Despite the tragic farce being played out at home, at least she was in her own environment. Now I was taking her into my world, a world in which I had lost my way. I wanted to reach out and take her hand to reassure her. But I didn't. I didn't want to offer her the strength I knew I didn't have. I hadn't yet learnt that the secret to true strength was to care for myself by caring more for others, especially those who loved me unconditionally and for whom I was responsible. All I knew that evening was that I couldn't embarrass Hilary any more than I already had. Somehow I would have to act the part for the next few hours. It's show time, I thought with grim humour as we entered the restaurant.

Kingsley saw us come in and made his way over to us with a wide grin on his face. "Mike, great to see you," he said enthusiastically, "and this must be Mrs Lipkin," he added warmly, shaking Hilary's hand. I introduced Hilary to him and she managed a wan smile. We stood there for a few moments as Kingsley pointed out the group of BBDG directors and their spouses standing in the corner a few metres away. "What happened to your face?" he asked, pointing to the cut underneath my eye. Hilary's eyes locked into mine. "I didn't see a protruding branch during my run through the park this evening," I replied, as Hilary looked down and shook her head.

The evening passed like a trance. The glamour and kudos of the dinner juxtaposed with the shame of the afternoon had short-circuited my emotions. I couldn't cross the enormous chasm between the two events and so I hung suspended somewhere in between. But somehow, my sensory overload and mild inebriation of a few Scotches too many released my rational self. In astonishment, I heard myself responding to questions and providing points of view that sounded like the Mike Lipkin of yesterday at his best. Hilary noted my performance and its effect on those around me with amazement. She knew though, just as I did, that I was incapable of sustaining this behaviour for any length of time. I had just demonstrated the classic inconsistency of a bipolar depressive. For those few precious moments, however, she felt the glow of pride and love that had characterised our first seven years together. While that evening provided little comfort, it gave us both a little hope because I had proved that I had not lost my faculties entirely. As Hilary would write later, it also made it that much harder for her to give up on me.

Looking back on that evening almost five years later, I still marvel at its chronology, happening as it did immediately after the afternoon before. I have long since ceased to believe in the concept of coincidence, the concept of random events that befall us as we make our way through this world. Instead, I believe in a higher logic that we may not always understand at the time but that always seems to make perfect sense if we try hard enough to understand it in retrospect. Life can only be understood backwards, but it must be lived forwards.

Although I didn't know it, despite my diseased state on that macabre day, I was already making progress. While I was still consumed by regret about the series of outlandish decisions I had made over the past year, I no longer asked the question: "Why is this happening to me?" I knew I was going through my torment because my values were based on the wrong premise. I knew I was selfish, I knew I pursued fraudulent goals, I knew I was feeling massively sorry for myself. I didn't know how to change, I didn't know when I would change, but I knew I had to change. It would take me another year and a half, though, to find the will and courage to do so.

The next four months were a blur of misery. Somehow I managed to perform adequately at BBDG for a few months before collapsing again. My fiasco at Ogilvy & Mather repeated itself as BBDG tried in vain to help me through the crisis. Eventually, in October, I was forced to resign, leaving myself unemployed and unemployable. By late 1990, the recession had hit Canada with a vengeance. Companies were downsizing with resultant massive staff layoffs. And so, as the first frigid winds of the winter of 1990 began to blow, I found myself standing along with thousands of other Canadians in the unemployment line for a government hand-out of a few hundred dollars a month. And yet, even though I had crashed professionally, I had rid myself of another illusion. After wrecking three jobs in quick succession, I no longer thought of myself as a high-powered professional. It didn't feel strange for me to be standing there. For the time being, I accepted where I was, but I had yet to discover how brutal life could be at the bottom of the food chain. Life had humbled me the way it does with anyone who is out of sync with its natural flow.

After living in my cousin's basement for a few weeks, I returned home. As much as they wanted to help, they couldn't shelter me indefinitely. Hilary took me back only because she knew I couldn't take care of myself any more. I now found it impossible to perform even the most rudimentary functions. However, she took me back more out of pity than out of love. It would be a long time before I would share her bed again. Instead, she made a room for me in the basement where I would spend more and more of my time cut off from reality and the rest of the world. She shielded me from the children as much as she could. All they knew was that Daddy was sick and that it would take a long time to make him well.

During this time, from May through November 1990, I saw my psychiatrist, Max Levy, twice a week. At first, he was extremely optimistic about my recovery. After all, he had witnessed me in my peak state during my time with AKL. As the weeks went by, however, he became increasingly frustrated with me. Neither the drugs he prescribed nor the psychotherapy he applied made any impact at all on my pathology. Finally, at the end of November, he said to me: "Michael, I can't seem to help you. Frankly, I don't believe anyone can help you because *I don't think you want to be helped.* Until you stop hating yourself and regretting what you have done, you will continue to suffer. Because now you're suffering over your suffering. I don't have the answers for you. Only you have those. I can't change your life for you, only you can. But you've got to break your negative thought pattern before you lose it all. I'm sorry, but I can't see you any more. I will provide you with the name of someone else who you can see. Maybe they *can* help you, but

I can't." As he finished talking, I thought of a psychiatrist joke a former client had told me, ignorant of the fact that I was in therapy. How many psychiatrists does it take to change a light bulb? Well, only one but it's expensive, it takes a long time and the light bulb has got to want to change.

Max Levy was right of course. I didn't want to help someone who disgusted me. I didn't want to help someone who was weak and out of control. I didn't want to help someone who represented everything I held in contempt. I didn't want to help me. As I left his office for the last time, I passed a panhandler in the street. "Can you spare some change, buddy?" he mumbled. As I looked at him, I thought of how easy it was to lose your dignity once you had lost your self-respect. There but for the grace of God go I, I used to murmur in thanks as I passed these unfortunate souls. Now I had virtually become one of them. If there are no depths to which the mind cannot fall, I was in freefall. The only difference between that panhandler and me was that I had a family who were not yet ready to consign me to the human scrapheap.

By mid-December, however, I had stretched my family past breaking point. The apparent futility of the situation became a big black blanket that smothered any relief from the ordeal. Hilary was on the verge of breakdown. Without my source of income, she had upped the number of hours she worked as a speech therapist for the local municipality to almost thirty hours a week. On top of that she was urgently trying to normalise life for the children and take care of her ill, self-abusive husband. To preserve her sanity, she made the decision to escape my madness by taking the kids to spend a month with her parents in South Africa. She also prayed that the shock of being completely alone might jolt me into recovery.

Exactly the opposite happened. During the next four weeks I ceased to function as a human being. Left alone in the house, I didn't wash. I hardly ate. With the last vestiges of responsibility I had left, I barely managed to feed the dog. All

I did was lie comatose on the couch from one day to the next, stirring only to buy cigarettes which I was now smoking at the rate of sixty a day. I became afraid to go outside because I'd lost the ability to interact with others. In fact, I had lost the ability even to think. My illness had progressed far enough to produce some of its most famous and sinister hallmarks: confusion, failure of mental concentration and lapse of memory. Everything seemed to be happening in slow motion. Even the voice in my head sounded like a vinyl record being played at half speed. Furthermore, what began as a mental malady had developed into a disease of mind *and* body. I pumped my body with so much toxin it's a miracle I didn't damage myself permanently.

It is inconceivable to those of healthy mind to understand the terrifying trauma of unbridled depression. Even the term, depression, implying as it does a kind of subdued mood, is completely the wrong epithet for the living nightmare that afflicts its victims. It is more like a mental cauldron that slowly cooks the senses, causing the most acute, almost physical pain.

And so I became a virtual hermit. The only two people I saw during the entire month were my brother-in-law, Leonard Preskow, who lived down the road, and my solitary friend, Mike Evans. I think they came to visit me every few days just to check whether I was still alive. It was Mike who suggested hospitalisation to me about a week before Hilary returned. I remember him saying to me as I lay on the couch: "You're dying, Mike. If you don't get some drastic treatment very quickly, I don't think you're going to make it."

Hilary returned to a ghost. I had lost over ten kilograms. I was suffering from exhaustion, the result of not being able to sleep for more than a couple of hours a night. The house also reflected the advanced stages of my disease: unkempt, chaotic, abused and abandoned. Even the dog seemed spooked as she crawled from out of her hiding place to greet Hilary and the kids. "No, no, no," was all Hilary could say again and again until it became a crazed, heart-rending wail.

In desperation, she called Mike Evans. Together they decided to admit me to the Richmond Hill Hospital, about ten kilometres north of where we lived.

I didn't even say goodbye to Carla and Anthony the following morning when Hilary and Mike Evans drove me to the hospital. Hilary had taken them to her sister-in-law to spare them the bewilderment of seeing their dad being taken away. As I sat in the back seat like a piece of human cargo, I felt totally flaccid. It was as though my spine had been removed, both mentally and physically.

Hilary and Mike sorted out the paperwork and I was ushered towards a cubicle where I was given a coarse, starched hospital gown to put on. A few minutes later, a nurse came by to take my blood pressure and feed me two bright orange pills, some kind of powerful sedative. Then an orderly placed my corpselike figure onto a movable bed with its faint smell of disinfectant and protective side bars. Until that moment, my drive towards self-destruction had had a weirdly romantic edge to it. I was uniquely significant, a rapidly upwardly mobile professional who was intent on committing hara-kiri. I had forsaken the fertile promise of my life for the badlands of my private emotional hell. Now I had become just another of life's endless casualties, a body on a stretcher with a little blue plastic bracelet featuring my name and patient number.

I was taken to a kind of holding area filled with other supine souls, waiting until they had cleared a bed for me in a ward upstairs. As the sedatives began to take effect, I felt strangely disembodied, as though I'd been placed in a halfway house between this world and the next. Suddenly I found myself moving. I remember the crinkly sound the bed's wheels made on the plastic tiles and the blurred images of people rushing past, all of them with a sense of purpose, a sense of sanity that had long since deserted me. And then, as though someone had focused a projector in my mind, I saw the face of my wife, blanched with disbelief and fright. She wasn't crying any more. The sight of her husband laid out like a cadaver had frozen her emotions. And yet, even in that moment of despair beyond despair, I felt the touch of her hand as she tried to give me one last squeeze of reassurance before they wheeled me away.

I was moved into the psychiatric ward of the hospital which was dedicated exclusively to victims of depression. At the time of my admission, there were approximately eighty in-patients, all suffering from the disease, the common cold of mental illness. They all seemed to be ordinary people who had taken one blow too many. I shared a ward with two other patients. The first was a 49-year-old architect who had tried to commit suicide because he had been retrenched from his company after 25 years' service. My second "wardmate" was a thirty-year-old Air Canada technician who was suffering severe anxiety attacks after working eighteen hours a day for the past six months, ironically to earn the overtime to pay off an overly large mortgage on a house he had bought but couldn't afford on his regular salary. Other patients included a nineteen-year-old girl with bandaged wrists whose boyfriend had left her and a fifty-year-old woman who had suffered recurring depressive episodes her entire adult life.

I had been placed in an environment where depression was the norm, but where adults were treated with the condescension reserved for the lame of mind. "And how are we feeling this morning?" was the first question I was asked by the nurse when I awoke the following day. I looked up to see a video camera which would track my every move for the next six weeks. In a rare moment of levity, I thought of the ward as a day and night care centre for adults behaving like children. Even the activities I would later perform were child-oriented.

Later that morning, a state-appointed psychiatrist came around to interview me and prescribe a cocktail of anti-depressants, anti-anxiety drugs and tranquillisers. It was clear that intensive psychotherapy would not be part of the treatment I would receive. This psychiatrist simply didn't have the time or the inclination to work intimately with me to achieve the breakthrough I so seriously needed. As disoriented as I was, I knew that the brightly coloured little pellets I held in my hand wouldn't help me. At best they would treat the symptoms and not the cause.

Now, as I think about all the people suffering from depression whom I have tried to counsel over the past three years since my recovery, I am amazed at how many of them regard medication as the cure-all. Drugs only mask the depression. In most cases, they do no more than simply help the sufferer cope with life while the depression runs its course. The fact is, depression often becomes a permanent companion while the drugs take the edge off the pain by taking the edge off life itself. After battling with the disease for almost three years, I believe that depression is pessimism turned inwards. It's pessimism in its advanced stages, where it has been allowed to permeate the spirit. And no pharmaceutical panacea can heal a soul in distress.

Despite my sterile, impersonal surroundings and my misgivings about the nature of my treatment at the hospital, I knew at that moment in my life I belonged where I was. For the time being I didn't have to think, I didn't have to confront a traumatised family, I could speak to other people just like me who had succumbed to the disease. I also knew that my hospitalisation was providing Hilary with a life-saving respite from me. For the next few weeks I submitted to the slow methodical rhythm of the treatment – awake at 7 a.m., breakfast at 8 a.m., support-group discussion at 9 a.m., lunch at 12 a.m., painting/drawing/puzzles/reading in the afternoon, followed by family visits at around 5 p.m. The psychiatrist would visit me twice a week to perfunctorily check my progress and adjust my medication. At first, I wasn't allowed outside. Then, once the staff were assured I wasn't suicidal, I was allowed to take walks unattended in the grounds around the hospital provided I signed out, indicating the time of departure.

Hilary would come and visit me every day. At first she came alone, later she would bring the kids. Our enforced separation probably saved our marriage. We could just sit and talk without the horror of her having to deal with my aberrational behaviour. By the beginning of the fourth week, the drugs also began to take effect. Although I felt sluggish, I also felt more relaxed. We could communicate without hysteria for the first time in almost ten months, and a tentative feeling of tenderness between us returned. It was also easier for the kids to deal with their dad's illness now that he was in hospital. Hilary had told them I was in hospital so the doctors could fix my brain which was broken. If you broke your arm or your leg you went to hospital, they reasoned, so why not your brain.

At the end of my fifth week in hospital something happened that brought me face to face with the full extent of my failure as a parent and human being. It was a Thursday morning at about 10.30 a.m. Instead of engaging in the mindlessly palliative morning activities, I had walked across to the main foyer of the hospital where I purchased a copy of the morning paper. I was sitting in a seat located against the wall reading when a group of grade two children and their teachers entered the hospital on a field trip. I suddenly saw my little girl in the group. Before I could hide behind my paper, our eyes met across the room. Instead of running across to greet me, however, her social survival instincts commanded her to ignore me. Even at that young age, she knew fathers weren't supposed to behave like hers was doing. I knew she didn't want to have to explain to her peers why her dishevelled dad was sitting in the hospital, with nothing visibly wrong with him, reading the paper.

As I slowly walked back to my ward in shame, my foreboding returned with a renewed ferocity. It was now the beginning of March 1991, almost two years since my first panic attack on that last Friday in June 1989. I knew that the preceding few weeks had been nothing more than a brief interlude in my drawn-out melodrama. While my raging anxiety seemed to be contained, I could only look at my future with terror. I had been unemployed for almost five months. My thoughts hung together like ill-fitting clothes. The drugs had made me even more lethargic than I was before I entered the hospital. Although outwardly I appeared to be more in control, I was stuffed with a sense of inner insecurity. I had zero faith in myself to get through the harrowing journey ahead. I realised one thing though: I would not convalesce in that place, I would only grow more infirm. That's why I put on a facade of recovery and convinced Hilary it was time for me to return home. A few days later, I checked myself out the hospital and headed back towards the abyss.

9

Coming Back

It's the day before the twins' seventh birthday. This is their third birthday since Michael started his journey to hell. He is currently in a psychiatric institution in Cedar Ridge, Kansas City, in America. It's the second time in six months that he's been hospitalised. The children are no longer five years old. They are older, wiser, more impressionable and vulnerable. When will the real Michael come back again? Will he ever come back again? Is the Michael I'm living with now the real Michael? Life is passing us by. I don't know what normal feelings are any more. I don't know what the difference is between being single and being married any more. I've been single for far too long and yet married at the same time. I cannot go on like this and yet I have to. I'm losing my passion for life.

HILARY LIPKIN'S DIARY, 23 SEPTEMBER 1991

When will life change for me? When will I wake up in the morning, smell the roses and greet the kids with a smile? The decision that is about to be made is to return to South Africa as a family and hopefully also to survive as one. What are the reasons why we would make such a move? Well,

1. To be close to family.
2. Love of the country.
3. Identification with the place.
4. A different perspective towards emigration because of the pain of the past two years.

5. *Michael regaining his self-esteem and a career.*
6. *King David School for the kids.*
7. *Grandparents for the kids.*
8. *Renewal of old acquaintances.*
9. *Liquifruit.*
10. *Tex bars.*
11. *Fleamarkets.*
12. *The weather.*
13. *Doing what my heart says is right.*
14. *Trying to save my marriage.*
15. *More emotional stability for Carla and Anthony.*

As the reality of returning to South Africa with Michael approaches, I am struck with an intense realisation: our wellbeing there depends on Michael's acceptance and desire to go back. At this stage he has neither. But then he doesn't know what he wants any more. I'm so exhausted by my inability to let go and leave him to function alone."

HILARY LIPKIN'S DIARY, 10 OCTOBER 1991

We have been back in South Africa since November last year. We stayed with my folks until our things arrived from Canada. We've just moved into a two-bedroom apartment in Sandton. Yet another physical move, yet another emotional adjustment. I finally rejected Michael outright. I cannot be around him any more. It's traumatic enough dealing with myself and the kids, I can't deal with his enormous burden any more. He is currently staying by himself in a flat up the road.

HILARY LIPKIN'S DIARY, 4 FEBRUARY 1992

I saw Michael this afternoon. He seems to have given up completely. He doesn't talk. He's isolated himself from society. He looks haunted, almost deranged. I don't think we even exist for him any more. It must be one of the most devastating experiences in life to see someone you love put themselves through a shredder without the resources to reconstruct. I'm not even angry with him any more, just terribly sad. I think he may have to be institutionalised. For the sake of the kids, I have to go on alone.

HILARY LIPKIN'S DIARY, 11 FEBRUARY 1992

To my Darling Mike.
I have been sending you Valentines for sixteen years and I'm not about to stop. Remember the one I made for you in Matric with the comic character and the red edges and the chain in the corner? Well, you still have a Valentine.

It's a long time since I've responded to you with care and tenderness. I do still feel an overwhelming love towards you, Michael, and I know you are still capable of loving.

You have been in a very bad time of your life for a very long time. But know that your wife and your children are still with you through all the pain even though we can't be together right now.

Don't give up your struggle. You have been blessed with a family that cares for the real person inside you. You are not a fake but you are also not an iron man. You are real. Forget about the flash and the pomp. Become a teacher to me, the kids and the world.

I need a husband. Carla and Anthony need a father. Come back to us, my love. Believe me when I tell you, you are a beautiful person. I know you better than anyone in the world. I know you will succeed in the fight against the demons who have possessed you. But I cannot do it for you. All I can guarantee you is my love. So on this Valentines Day, I shower you with the brightest white light possible.

Fight back, Michael. You are not useless. Your life is not over. We are young and vibrant. Your children are too small not to have a father. Reach out for your soul. Clean the aura around you. Emerge from all of this stronger than before.

You have no choice. Don't let this be the last Valentine you receive. That would be a cruel choice.

Love and kisses, Hil XXX

HILARY LIPKIN'S VALENTINE CARD TO MIKE LIPKIN, 14 FEBRUARY 1992

For the first few weeks after I returned home from hospital, I was like a tame rabbit released into the wild. Almost everything threatened me. I was terrified to drive any more, especially after colliding with the curb one night on my home from the mall where I used to spend my days wandering around. Even the simple act of going to Hilary's sister for dinner intimidated me. I had to watch Hilary to see which knife and fork to use. From someone who used to make a living out of talking, I had become almost mute. The truth was, I had become so embroiled in my own psychological struggle that I had ceased to relate to other adults, but this did not apply to children. Ironically, I began to relate better to Carla and Anthony, as I was operating on their level.

In fascination, I watched myself withdraw further and further from reality. Although I seemed to have lost the power to control my behaviour, this ability to observe and judge myself from a distance had stayed with me during the entire two-year ordeal. I learnt later that the presence of a second being – wraithlike, powerless yet objective – was a distinctive mark of the depression experience. Time and time again in my conversations with people still afflicted by the disease, I hear the agonised cry: "But this is not me!" The "other self" is who they believe they truly are, not the physical person floundering in pathos. Like so many others, the discordance between the ethereal and the external being was the fountainhead of my pain.

I believe that my "other self" was my higher self. But I had ignored it for my entire adult life. My depression was therefore an inevitability waiting to happen. It was a poignant recognition that my soul was being ignored. Its demands were out of sync with the demands of my personality, the sum total of my physical, mental, emotional and social traits. In fact, until the onset of my depression, I was not even aware of my higher self. I believed I *was* my personality, which could only be satisfied through the pursuit of sensual, status and financial goals. Incredibly, these were the realisations I was making while outwardly losing my way. That's why I cringe when I hear the word "breakdown" associated with depression, implying as it does a kind of moral frailty. If anything, it was a moral clarification. But the force of my experience had taken my head apart. I knew I would never be the same again. Back then, though, like Humpty Dumpty, I'd had a great fall and I didn't know how to put myself back together again.

As the months passed, I made a half-hearted attempt at a series of ad hoc jobs ranging from trying to sell magazine subscriptions by phone to hawking water-purifier systems to businesses. Each failure reinforced my hopelessness. My glittering former career in advertising seemed like part of a previous lifetime. It had been so long since I'd exercised my intellect that even the dinner with the directors of BBDG a year previously seemed like a fantasy. The more ineffectual I became, the more obsessed I became about what I had thrown away. "If only, if only, if only," the eternal lament of the has-been became my constant refrain. If only I hadn't taken so much for granted. If only I could get my focus back. If only I wasn't such an asshole. If only . . .

By August 1991, my mental deterioration was so massive that I seemed to have physically metamorphosised. One Sunday morning, I was taking shelter in the past by browsing through a photo album containing pictures from our early years in Canada before the depression hit. The vital, youthful face that smiled at me repeatedly off the page bore very little resemblance to the haggard, lifeless visage that now scowled at me every morning. My entire body from the face down seemed to have sagged in resignation. More than anything else though, it was the eyes which had changed. They had no light, no love, no life.

Since my hospitalisation, I had ceased taking any form of medication and I had stopped seeing a psychiatrist. Physically, I believed I had proven to myself that unlike many other sufferers of depression, drugs could not even ameliorate my condition. Intellectually, I knew there would be no earth-shattering realisations that would lead me back to health. I didn't get any relief or comfort any more by talking about myself to a professional listener. I was so fatigued and frustrated that I couldn't bear hearing my own voice droning on and on about my predicament. I was caught in limbo, between the perceived glory of my past and abject fear of my future.

I used to oscillate between apathy and agitation. I'd lie lifeless on my bed in the basement and then be suddenly assaulted by a panic attack so ferocious that I would pace frantically up and down the house for hours. The length of the panic attacks grew to the point where I was in a state of permanent delirium. I couldn't call Max Levy any more, so in desperation I visited the Ontario Mental Health Centre in downtown Toronto. I told the psychiatrist on duty, Dr John Patterson, about the events leading up to my abortive hospitalisation in February and my disintegration since. I told him I was suicidal because I didn't know how much longer I could endure the pain. He immediately prescribed a tranquilliser and then asked me whether I thought I could make it through the next 24 hours. He needed to contact Richmond Hill Hospital and explore all the treatment options open to him, he said. I nodded and he asked me to return the following afternoon.

When I returned the next day, Patterson told me he had spoken with the staff at Richmond Hill Hospital and reviewed my employment record in Canada. "You are obviously a highly intelligent, capable person whose faculties have been impaired by this depressive episode," he said with monumental understatement. "However, based on your achievements and your future potential for recovery, we have decided to send you to the Cedar Ridge Clinic in Kansas City for treatment. Cedar Ridge specialises in stress-related disorders. It is a fine facility and I'm sure they will be able to help you. Your plane leaves tomorrow night at 8 p.m. and you can collect your ticket at the airport. There will also be someone to collect you when you arrive in Kansas City."

Eleven-thirty p.m., 22 August 1991. An orderly processed

my admittance to Cedar Ridge Clinic. I was so disoriented that I couldn't even remember my phone number. He asked me for my toiletry bag and removed my razor. For the entire length of my stay, someone would observe me every morning while I shaved. Then he led me to my ward which I shared with one other patient. Although it was past midnight, my wardmate was still wide awake. "What they got you in for, man?" he asked with an accent so thick I could barely understand him. He was a wiry, highly strung young black man who seemed to be jumping about even though he was sitting on his bed. I looked at him dumbly. "Hey, man, they got me for sniffing coke on the assembly line. Only problem was I sniffed a bit too much. My name is Jeb Kenner," he continued as he held out his hand to shake mine. He went on to tell me that he was an auto worker on the General Motors Chevrolet assembly line in Tennessee. His coke habit had reached the point where his performance at work was impaired. General Motors had sent him to Cedar Ridge for drug rehabilitation. What the hell am I doing in a drug-rehabilitation centre, I wondered to myself in utter perplexity.

I discovered the following morning that Cedar Ridge was divided into two sections – a stress-disorder clinic and a drug-rehabilitation centre. By mistake, I had been admitted to the drug-rehabilitation centre. It was a bizarre introduction to another five weeks of futile treatment. But I knew that the treatment would be ineffectual even before I arrived. I had become a fugitive from life and Cedar Ridge was my hiding place. At the end of September, I could hide no longer. And so I returned home, stuck in a rut that seemed to grow deeper with every passing day.

By the beginning of October, despite Hilary's Herculean efforts, our financial reserves were almost depleted. I had been unemployed for almost a year. Even my half-hearted attempts at earning a living between hospitalisations had brought in barely more than a minimum wage. My future prospects were even bleaker. The constant misery and tension at home was also beginning to take its toll on the kids. The teachers had called Hilary to tell her that both children appeared listless in class. Anthony was also lagging behind his classmates in his grades and he was engaging in uncharacteristic emotional outbursts. I listened, sick with guilt, as Hilary told me what the school social worker had advised her: our children were displaying typical symptoms of severe family-related stress.

Two weeks later, we made the decision to return to South Africa. Or rather, Hilary made the decision and I reluctantly acknowledged that there was no alternative but to go back. In South Africa, Hilary and the kids would have the support of her parents while I could begin again if I could find the will to begin again. I rallied myself sufficiently to call my alma mater, Ogilvy & Mather, in Johannesburg to procure a job. I lied about why I was returning to South Africa, stating that we were returning because of the opportunities being generated by the changes taking place there. On the strength of my stellar achievements prior to emigration, I negotiated a senior position with the company, which would entail managing the agency's largest account. We sold the house, the cars and the appliances and then held a garage sale of all our other possessions we wouldn't be taking with us. As I watched strangers poke about our goods strewn about our driveway, I felt like a moribund animal having its entrails eaten by scavengers.

I still have nightmares about our last few days in Canada. Hilary and I stayed in the basement of her friend's house while the children stayed with her sister-in-law. I had arrived four-and-a-half years earlier on a magic carpet woven of hope, energy, talent, money and youth. I was returning broken in mind, body and spirit. Forty-eight hours before we flew back to South Africa, the convulsions started as the full magnitude of my perverse achievement assaulted me. The energy surges were so violent and so negative that I found myself running wildly up and down the streets punching trees and lampposts in self-directed rage and fury, oblivious to the stunned stares of passers-by. I know that if a policeman had seen me, I would have been arrested and sent home in a straightjacket. In panic, Hilary called Ian, our friend and family doctor, who immediately prescribed Ativan, a powerful anti-anxiety and tranquillising drug. And that's how I left Canada, half mad and heavily sedated.

On 15 November 1991, we boarded the first South African Airways direct flight from New York to Johannesburg since the lifting of sanctions. It was an auspicious signal. After almost two-and-a-half years of pathology, I was headed towards recovery, although compared to what I would go through over the next three-and-a-half months, my Canadian experience was merely a supporting act.

As I stepped out of the plane onto the tarmac at Jan Smuts Airport, I thought that I had simply swopped one horror show for another. Coming back to South Africa to resettle after being away for almost five years was like emigrating to a new country all over again. The glaring heat of the Highveld summer sun after the frigid Canadian autumn, the parched landscape, the alien sounds of the vernacular – both Afrikaans and Black – all converged to blow my disoriented mind. Driving along the M1, I looked at the mine dumps and thought that if Toronto was one of the most civil cities in the world, Johannesburg must rank as one of its harshest. It was still an acquisitive, gold-mining town, not a place for the faint-hearted or clinically depressed.

As we stopped at a traffic light near Hilary's parents' house where we would spend the next two months, my eyes met those of a dancing flower vendor waving his fistfuls of pink, yellow and crimson. He appeared to be about my age, but his rugged, handsome features contrasted incongruously with his torn T-shirt and shapeless shoes. He thrust his technicolor merchandise through the window. "Hey, Nkosi, only R5 a bunch!" he shouted at me with a disarming grin of dazzling teeth. I just looked at him uncomprehendingly for a few seconds before he sprinted towards the sound of a hooter a few cars away. Where does he find that smile inside of him, I marvelled, as I thought of my own mournful temperament. He had nothing but his spirit was full. I had everything but I had nothing inside. I didn't know it then, but that flower vendor and the thousands of others like him would become the role models that sustained my recovery.

We moved in with Hilary's parents, but I wasn't grateful for their hospitality, I was humiliated. All I could think about was that at the age of thirty-four I was thoroughly dependent on someone else to take care of me and my family. I thought nostalgically about the heated debates about politics and business I had conducted with David, Hilary's father, over a decade before while I was still courting Hilary. I remembered the amusement and affection I had seen in his eyes. Now, I imagined that all I saw was pity and scorn. It wasn't, of course. It was an immense tenderness and shared pain. But when the mind is poisoned, everything looks rotten. We are our thoughts. True "reality" is inside our heads. The words we use to describe our experiences become our experiences. My mental storm had been raging for so long that there was nothing left but a landscape of bitterness and battered dreams where nothing good could grow.

A week later, I started my job at Ogilvy & Mather, Johannesburg. They were thrilled, believing that they had hired one of the hottest talents in South African advertising. My appointment was the culmination of a six-month search for someone with the skills to manage a complex piece of business worth about R5 million in annual income to the company. "This is it, Mike. If you screw this one up, you're fucked," I said to myself as I was introduced to the client and my team on the account. I knew that I had a few weeks of breathing space to acclimatise myself. I took some weak comfort from the fact that the agency was already winding down for the December holiday season and I wasn't expected to really demonstrate my leadership until the new year. My idea of long-term planning at that stage was just getting through the day, so January 1992 seemed like an eternity

110

away. What's more, in comparison to my predecessor on the account who had been perceived as abrasive and arrogant, my introverted behaviour was interpreted as mature humility by my new colleagues. Nothing was what it seemed, everything was a mirage.

A couple of days before Christmas, I was introduced to the typical South African's attitude towards depression. I had gone on a field trip with the client to visit some of his stores in the Gauteng area. As we drove from one town to another, he became increasingly agitated, shaking his head and muttering to himself. "What's wrong, Bill?" I asked him. He looked at me, unsure of whether to share the source of his disquiet or not. Eventually, he lit a Dunhill and said to me: "It's my wife, Mike. I don't know what to do any more. She's got everything. I make good money. Our kids are great. But she was admitted to the Morningside Clinic yesterday for what the doctors call 'depression'. This is the second time it's happened. The worst thing is, she won't talk to me about it. How can I help her if I don't even know why she feels like she does? The doctors tell me it's something physical but I think that's bullshit. I wish she'd just get herself together instead of feeling sorry for herself all the time. I can't take it any more. If she carries on like this, I'm going to leave her."

Bill's ignorant words of contempt would become a chorus in the months ahead. I would hear the phrase "just pull yourself together" many times before my recovery in February 1992. And every time I heard it, I would slide further into the mire. Those are the most destructive words you can say to a person in the grip of depression, because you are simply reminding them of their impotence. As a tragic aside, Bill did leave his wife, unable to come to terms with her condition. She committed suicide in September 1992. He has since remarried and I saw him again in June 1994. By this time he had read my story in *Style* magazine, and knew therefore that I had been in the same place as his former wife back in the summer of '91. He had become a very different man with a very different attitude towards the disease of depression. As a human being, he had learnt what being human could mean.

Together with Hilary's parents, we flew down to Cape Town after Christmas for ten days. It had been almost eight years since I was there last. In that time, I had travelled all over the world, but nowhere else I visited held the staggering beauty of this place between Devil's Peak and the deep blue sea. Every wave seemed to recharge my ailing spirit. As I watched my children frolic in the surf off Llandudno beach beneath an azure sky, I felt a delicious rush of *joie de vivre*. Maybe, just maybe, I could beat the bogeyman who had become my constant antagonist.

To no avail. My fragile sense of wellbeing was shattered the moment I returned to work to confront my moment of truth. My period of grace was over. It was time to deliver. With a sickening sense of *déjà vu*, I started to go through the motions again. But I had neither the passion nor the predisposition to perform my assigned task. My depression was like a virus that had wiped out my knowledge base. I couldn't even rise to the occasion for brief moments any more. In a business driven by hot-blooded emotion and enthusiasm, I was about as animated as an adder in the Arctic.

About ten days after we'd arrived back, Hilary and I had begun seeing a psychologist, Dr Ann Silk, recommended to us by one of our acquaintances who had recently beaten depression. She had a wonderfully gentle presence and a way of articulating my plight that soothed my psyche, albeit only for the two hours a week I spent with her in her office. By this stage, Hilary needed a therapist as much as I did. She began to see Silk on her own. Unlike me, however, Hilary never lost her will to keep moving forwards. She was determined to get through the storm intact. For the first time, she discovered someone to whom she could relate. In Ann Silk she had found her guide and support. Partially as a result of Silk's reinforcement, Hilary finally insisted that we physically separate. The confined space of a small condominium in Sandton which had been our home since mid-

January had exacerbated the tension between us. There was nowhere for her to avoid my debilitating presence and so she put some distance between us by finding me a tiny apartment a few kilometres away.

By the middle of January, Silk decided that I was beyond her help. In an interview I conducted with her in June 1994 during the course of writing this book, this is what she told me: "My impression of you when I first saw you was that you were a bright and thinking person. That gave me tremendous hope in terms of your potential to grow, evolve, overcome. But as I worked with you in our first few sessions, I could see how incredibly entrenched your thought processes were. Unlike Hilary who wanted to move forward, you were locked into the past so tightly that none of the positive hopefulness I was feeling could touch you. I realised at that point that you were not ready for re-evaluation, for setting new goals, for restructuring your beliefs. I knew that you needed something very extreme to release you from your 'stuckness' and that didn't fall within my field of expertise. In fact, I felt that you were on the edge of psychosis. You were disconnected from reality, very close to disintegration. That's why I referred you to Frank Carp [a psychiatrist] who would be able to apply more drastic drug therapy and psychotherapy.

"I felt I could be of far more help to Hilary at the time because she didn't know how to hold it all together," Silk continued. "She was experiencing the confusion of revulsion, rage, anger and pity overlaid on her love for you which she never, ever lost. I felt she needed to express all those emotions to a supportive person so she didn't explode at home."

As Hilary and I sat in Frank Carp's rooms waiting to see him for the first time, I thought of how futile the past three years had been. I thought of that moment with Hilary in Dr Haines's rooms so long ago in Toronto. I thought of how many chances I had been given to break my vicious spiral and how I had almost purposely thrown them all away. I thought: I've finally reached my last cul-de-sac. I've forced my family to return in the vain hope I could heal myself. But I can't, it's hopeless. They'll be better off without me. If only I could just crawl away and die and release them from my misery. I was cocooned in blackness, blind to anything but the swirl of shadows in my head.

When I met Frank Carp, we recognised each other immediately. We had completed our officers' training together during our compulsory military service thirteen years before. He was a gentle giant of a man with kind, almost babylike features. He was soft-spoken, with an endearing habit of tilting his head slightly to the side when he listened to you. Silk had briefed him thoroughly on my condition and throughout the session he consulted his notes. Like Dr Haines, he first directed most his questions to Hilary. Then he turned to me and listened to my disjointed narrative. After almost two hours, he said to us: "Michael, I think you are experiencing a severe schizoid episode." What the hell did that mean, I thought, as I saw Hilary frown uncomprehendingly. "What that means," Carp continued, seeing our bemused expressions, "is that you are suffering from a personality disorder marked by depression, dissociation from reality, passivity and withdrawal. Your self-identity has eroded to the point where I believe you don't know who you are any more. I am going to try help you with medication and intensive therapy but you may need to be hospitalised." I'm going to spend the rest of my life in and out of hospitals, I thought to myself in shock.

Carp had consciously decided not to candy-coat his diagnosis. After all the abortive therapy I'd already been through, he didn't want to offer us any false hope of a recovery he couldn't deliver. Instinctively, I knew that what he was telling us was true. Curiously, I was also consoled by his words. I didn't have to take responsibility for my actions if I was so seriously ill. After all, hadn't Carp just told me that I was a heartbeat away from insanity? No wonder I was feeling so fucked. For Hilary, however, Carp's words were a confirmation of her most savage fear. We had travelled fifteen thousand kilometres back to a place far worse than where we were before we started. At least in Canada she was functioning. She had made a life for herself. Now she could only wait in trepidation for the next chapter in my surreal saga.

I reached the point at Ogilvy & Mather where I no longer even pretended to do my job any more. I would come in at 9 a.m., lock my door and sit silently at my desk until 5 p.m. when I would leave. I felt as if I was drowning in lethargy. Some days, even the act of remaining vertical was an impossible effort, so I would lie down on the carpet and drift into a half-conscious state. The only decision I would make during the day was which brand of cigarette to chain-smoke – Winston or Benson and Hedges. I maintained this charade because Hilary still had the illusion that somehow I was still working. She knew that if I lost my job at the agency, all was lost.

The dreadful dilemma of a depressive is the dichotomous inability to relate to other people on the one hand, and the inability to be alone on the other. As bad as it was for me during the day, the prospect of returning to an empty cubicle at night was even worse. I didn't even have a TV in my flat to help me flee from myself. My only refuge was sleep, but despite medication even that had largely eluded me. Then one day just before the end of January, I received a call from someone who would become my lifeline during my final month of madness. If it hadn't been for him, I'm not sure I would have made it. Saviours appear at the most improbable times in the most unlikely guises.

Howard Roth was a close friend of mine from school but the last time I had seen him was in 1978 when we completed our B. Comm. at Wits together. In the years since then, he had been an even more successful yuppie than me. He made millions through his energy and extraordinary financial flair before he too was consumed by depression halfway through 1990. Like me, Roth had imploded. He had been

115

hospitalised five months before, his wife had left him and he was forced to declare personal bankruptcy. Unlike me, however, Roth had begun to inch his way back to health. He had found a job with a small but highly rated investment company who were helping him rediscover his natural acumen. Roth's brother was married to a friend of Hilary's and that's how he found out about my plight.

"Listen, my china," he said to me, "I believe you're going through some deep *kuk*. My *boet* told me what's happened to you. I know what you're going through because I've been there. Let's talk." He told me briefly about his experiences over the past two years and then suggested we meet for drinks after work. That night we both found a soul mate. It was the first time either one of us had spoken to anyone who genuinely understood the other's agony. As I spoke, Roth nodded his head in empathy. In return, when Roth spoke, he seemed to be describing my misadventure. Roth was still single and not yet ready for another relationship. He also shared my phobia about being alone, so we resolved to help each other through the crisis by forming a two-person support group. Over the next few weeks, we saw each other frequently.

Looking back, it was Roth who really inspired me to write my first article for *Style* magazine. He pierced my isolation by showing me that I was not the only member of the human race ever to go through the horror of depression. The mere discovery that I was not alone in my experience provided me with enormous relief. While I would remain disabled during the day, at least I could look forward to escaping the demons at night.

At the beginning of February, top management at Ogilvy & Mather decided to confront me about my weird behaviour and total incompetence at work. Alan Bunton, the group managing director and my previous mentor at Grey Phillips, was given the unenviable assignment of speaking to me. It was a session filled with mutual pain. My relationship with Bunton went far deeper than business. The time we had spent together at Grey Phillips in the eighties was a high point of both our lives. In many respects I had modelled my style on his. He had given me air cover to do almost anything I wanted at Grey and, in return, I walked through fire for him. He was one of the major reasons why Ogilvy & Mather had hired me in the first place. Now I sat before him as a mental and emotional quadriplegic.

I relived my confession to Pam Magen at Ogilvy & Mather in Toronto in August 1989 as I told Bunton the truth about what had happened to me over the past three years and my diseased state of mind at that moment. I stopped just short of Carp's diagnosis to me a few days before. He listened in silence, shaking his head in disbelief. "I knew something was obviously wrong," he said eventually, "but I had no idea it was this serious. I promise you we'll do everything we can to get you through this. I know what you're made of. I know you'll make it." He asked me whether it was okay for him to call both Hilary and Frank Carp. I nodded and he promised to come back to me the following day with the agency's plan of action. That afternoon, he called Carp to find out more about my condition and to ask for advice about how to handle me. Then he called Hilary to tell her that the company knew about what was going on. He reassured her that they would support me and told her to call him any time, day or night, if she needed his help or if she just wanted to talk.

When I entered my office the following morning, there was a note on my desk to see Bunton. It said to ask his secretary to call him out of his board meeting as soon as I came in. I called her and within minutes Bunton walked into my office. He closed the door, sat down and said: "We want you to devote all your energy to getting well without distressing yourself about work. That's why we've decided to relieve you of your account management responsibilities for as long as it takes you to get better." Bunton noted my anguished expression in response to his words and continued: "Mike, it's nothing to be ashamed of. I think many of us have been

117

close to where you are at some point in our lives. As you know, I went into the bush for extended periods to get myself back on track. At the moment, you're not well and you need to heal yourself. We'll send a note out to the staff telling them that you've had a change in assignment. From now until you're better you'll be 'working' on new business development and special projects. Neil Hamann will take over your portfolio and we'd appreciate it if you could brief him later this morning. I spoke to Hilary yesterday so I know about your domestic situation. She's an amazing woman, Mike. She really loves you. And you've got a lot of friends here who want to see you back on your feet again."

I have tried to record that conversation with Bunton as accurately as I can remember it, because I think it's an exemplar of how to talk to a person in depression. Bunton demonstrated just the right degree of support, empathy and understanding. He didn't admonish me "to pull myself together", but at the same time he let me know that there were people depending on me and that it was my responsibility to heal myself.

When I think back to that stormy period in my life, I am still in awe of the remarkable acts of kindness performed by so many people towards me. While I was losing myself, I was finding out the best part of being human – a sense of caring and consideration for your fellow man or woman. The truth is, altruism pays. Giving replenishes you. The more you give the more you have to give, not only to others but also to yourself. As Gandhi said: "Service is the rent you pay for living here. All that is not given is lost." Back at the beginning of February 1992, though, I hadn't yet learnt how even to receive kindness. And so my malnourished spirit continued to weaken.

"So you're going to throw this job away as well," Hilary said to me in tears of rage and helplessness. She had come to visit me in my flat after her conversations with Alan Bunton. "I know we're going to go through the whole nauseating process again, aren't we? I should have told Alan

Bunton not to worry about trying to help you because you're determined to screw it up again, aren't you? Well, why don't you save us all a lot of trouble and just end it now. That's what you want, isn't it?" I couldn't even look at her any more. Her desperate anger made me want to gag on my inadequacy. I could only rub my sweaty palms together and rock autistically in my seat.

"Oh, Michael," she said kneeling before me, as rage gave way to resignation, "I'm sorry for losing my temper with you. I know you can't help it but I'm so exhausted from all of this. Will it ever end? Will you ever come back to us?" I couldn't answer her so I continued to hide behind an expressionless silence.

By the middle of February, it became apparent that Carp's prognosis was right. Medication and therapy were never going to help me. My last session with him convinced him that I would have to be hospitalised. By that stage I was unable to tell the difference between mental and physical pain any more, because my mental anguish *was* so acutely physical. The only way I could cope with my meltdown was to remain entirely passive. I had learnt to turn my mind into an amoeba, to blur my thoughts so they had no shape whatsoever. But every now and then, a ghoulish reality would gate-crash my ruminations, sending me into a convulsion where I would literally writhe around on the floor. In response to Carp's probing, that's exactly what happened to me in his office.

"Michael," he said to me after I'd calmed down, "I'm booking you into Tara. I know the people there. It's an excellent facility. They'll be able to give you the attention you need." TARA!!! The very name filled me with terror. From early childhood, every Johannesburg child had grown up with expressions of exasperation like "I'm going to end up in Tara" or "You'll end up in Tara" or "You're sending me to Tara". Now I was going there for real. While I was still in his office, Carp called his contact at Tara. After a brief conversation, he put the phone down and told me that a bed would be available for me in five days' time. "It's over," I thought with terminal abdication. "I'll die in that place. But I've got nowhere else to go. I can't think for myself any more and I can't cope with the real world. If Carp says that's where I'm going then that's where I'm going to have to go. If only I had the guts to end it all now."

It ain't over till it's over, the saying goes. Fate decided to throw me one last ball. A friend of ours, Lianne Rabner, was related to Dr Brian Lamb, one of South Africa's leading psychiatrists and pharmacologists. Two days before I was due to check into Tara, she suggested I see him for a second opinion. It was the beginning of the beginning.

10

You're so Beautiful!

I spoke to Brian yesterday after Mike's first shock treatment. All he would tell me is that it was too soon to notice whether there was any improvement or not. He said Mike was heavily sedated and asleep most the time so it would be pointless for me to visit him.

After the second treatment today, Brian indicated that he believes there may be a slight improvement. He said I should visit Mike tomorrow because there will be a day's break before the third treatment. For me, it's impossible after all this time to imagine any improvement at all. I can't muster any enthusiasm or optimism. I'm so nervous. I don't know what to expect. Has he made any progress? Or will I just be let down again?

HILARY LIPKIN'S DIARY, 23 FEBRUARY 1992

I went to see Mike today. He's in a room with three other guys who are also receiving shock therapy. When I came into the room, I saw him sleeping in the corner bed. He seemed so peaceful. I just wanted to hug him, it's been so long since I did that. He opened his eyes and said, "Oh hi, Hil". Do you know, he actually smiled! I told him not to try and talk. I said I just wanted to be with him. Then he dozed off again. I don't know whether it's the sedatives but he seems more relaxed than I've ever seen him. For the first time, I'm daring to hope again. I'm exhausted.

HILARY LIPKIN'S DIARY, 24 FEBRUARY 1992

I visited Mike this afternoon after his third treatment this morning. When I arrived, he was sleeping so I just sat by the bed and watched him. When he woke up, he asked me if I would help him take a bath. He looked at me and squeezed my hand. I know something's different. His eyes . . . they've got their life back. I felt a surge of love for him rush through me. I know he's going to be okay. I know I was right to stick with him.

I helped him bath and shave. He was still a bit shaky from the sedatives and the anaesthetic. I sat with him while he ate dinner in Minerva's cute little dining room. He even offered me some food. I'm absolutely shaking with excitement. I think I'm witnessing a miracle.

I phoned Brian as soon as I got home. I'm so excited and he's so calm. He reassured me again that the treatment seems to be working. There's just one more session to go.

HILARY LIPKIN'S DIARY, 25 FEBRUARY 1992

I took the kids with me to fetch Mike this morning. It was absolutely amazing. When we got there he wasn't lying on his bed any more. We found him in the garden. He looked incredible. He just radiated happiness. He hugged Carla and Anthony for about five minutes. And then he kissed and hugged me. All he kept saying to us was "You're so beautiful!" I didn't think I would ever live to see this day. It is a miracle. I know the nightmare is finally over.

HILARY LIPKIN'S DIARY, 27 FEBRUARY 1992

Eleven a.m., 21 February 1992. Hilary drove me to my first meeting with Brian Lamb. His office was located in an outbuilding behind his house. We were ushered in by his receptionist and told that Brian would be with us in a moment. One side of the room was entirely lined with books, a couple written by Brian himself. Clay sculptures also crafted by Brian had been placed around the room. After all the psychiatrists' rooms I had been in over the previous three years, this one felt different – less impersonal, less clinical. The room had a feeling which soothed me even before I met Lamb.

"Hi, Michael," I heard a cultured voice say as I peered out of the window into the garden. I turned to see Brian Lamb for the first time. He had a face that belonged somewhere in the Old Testament, with a white beard and an equally white mane of hair that tumbled over his bushy eyebrows. He sat down in front of me and looked at me intently with dark, probing eyes. For the first time, I got the feeling that I was being observed as a person, not as a patient. "You know, I was a friend of your mother," he said. "I used to do tai chi with her. I also admired her work very much." Instead of distancing himself, Lamb had immediately personalised the relationship.

"Lee has told me about you," Brian continued. "She tells me they want to put you in Tara. She says you've been stuck in depression for almost three years. Tell me how you're feeling right now." I seemed to slur my thoughts as my words came stumbling out. Suddenly, after I'd been speaking for about fifteen minutes, Lamb said decisively: "I know how to get you out of this. I'm going to prescribe electro-convulsive therapy to break your entrenched negative thought patterns." I conjured up a vision of being strapped down on a table with electrodes taped to my temples as my body was being electrocuted. "First Tara, now this barbarous treatment," I thought numbly as I glanced at Hilary, who was visibly shaken. Scenes from *One Flew over the Cuckoo's Nest* flapped around in my head.

The reality is that electro-convulsive therapy (ECT) is a much-maligned and falsely feared treatment which is really remarkably safe. In his book, *Depression and How To Survive It*, Anthony Clare writes that ECT is vilified by critics who in truth often know little about it, while it is praised by many patients who have found it a lifeline to recovery. I didn't know it then, but I was about to count myself among the latter. Clare goes on to quote an excerpt from an account of ECT published in the 1965 *British Journal of Psychiatry* by a psychiatrist who had received a course of treatment for depression. The article was written with the hope that it would *dispel the myth that ECT is a terrifying form of treatment, crippling in its effects on the memory and in other ways. The technique is today so refined that the patient suffers a minimum of discomfort, and the therapeutic benefits are so great in those cases where it is indicated that it is a great pity to withhold it from mistaken ideas of kindness to the patient.*

Obviously ECT doesn't work for everybody, but for those suffering from severe depression it can be very effective. It is at least as good as antidepressant drugs, says Clare, and it acts more rapidly. In my case, I had proved over an extended period that antidepressant drugs were entirely ineffectual in combating my affliction. Lamb understood that fact immediately.

Clare, who counts Spike Milligan among his patients, states that it is the induced convulsion caused by ECT that appears to bring about the antidepressant effect. Like depression itself, it is not known precisely how ECT works, but it is believed that it acts on those neurotransmitters in the brain believed to hold the key to severe depression. Another possibility is that ECT works by its effects on those centres in the brain that regulate the body's circadian rhythms, rhythms which are upset in depression. Finally, ECT may also work by impacting on those hormones whose secretion is altered in depression. Lamb explained the action of ECT as follows: like a heart which has gone into cardiac arrest sometimes requires an electric shock to activate it again, so it is with certain parts of the brain. All I understood was that I had been trapped in my pathological thought patterns for so long that I literally needed to be shocked out of them.

Clare describes the administration of ECT as follows: the patient is not allowed food for four hours prior to the anaesthetic to rule out the danger of vomiting while under its influence. The patient then lies on a bed with the pillow removed. He or she is then given an intravenous injection of a short-acting anaesthetic and, through the same needle, a dose of muscle relaxant. Within 15–20 seconds of the injection, muscle paralysis is imminent and the anaesthetist takes over respiration of the patient by way of a face mask and pressure bag. When the patient is well-oxygenated by means of the mask and bag (skin colour good, blood pressure and pulse steady), the shock can be safely administered.

Two electrodes, dampened with a bicarbonate solution to prevent skin burns at their point of contact, are applied to the scalp at each side of the head, above and in front of each ear. A gag is placed in the patient's mouth to prevent the tongue from being accidentally bitten.

Modern ECT machines deliver a string of high voltage, very brief, direct current pulses, about 60–70 pulses a second, which results in a "modified" convulsion. After the convulsion, the gag is removed and the patient is turned on one side. The anaesthetist maintains an oxygen supply until the muscle relaxant wears off and the patient starts to breathe on his own. Within five to twenty minutes the patient returns to full consciousness, although he or she may feel sleepy and indeed may sleep for up to an hour after treatment. The usual course of treatment consists of between six and twelve treatments. I would only go through a course of four treatments before Brian decided I had been healed.

"I want you to take Mike home now and pack his bags," Lamb said to Hilary on that momentous morning of 21 February 1992, "then I want you to drive him to the Minerva Clinic in Bezuidenhout Valley. By 2.30 p.m., they will have a bed ready for him. And don't worry, ECT is perfectly safe. I wouldn't recommend it if I wasn't completely certain of that fact." Then he looked at me and said with absolute conviction: "I am going to heal you. In one week's time you'll discover yourself again." There was something about Brian and the assurance with which he said those words to me that ignited a tiny flicker of hope in my gut. But what he was promising me was a miracle and I had lost all faith in the possibility of miracles. Lamb recognised the extent of my hopelessness, because when I asked him after my recovery why he had acted with such urgency, he told me: "I didn't know how much time I had. You were among the worst cases of severe depression I had ever seen. Who knows what you could have done, but I wasn't going to take a chance."

The Minerva Clinic in Bezuidenhout Valley was a stone's throw from where I grew up in Yeoville. On our way to the clinic we passed an old barbershop where I used to have my hair cut almost twenty years before. On a whim, I said to Hilary: "I want to shave my hair off." I felt as if the ECT I was about to undergo was a ritual that would either recharge or ruin me. As crazy as it may now seem, having my hair shaved off then seemed like an imperative act of humility. It was my way of preparing myself mentally for what was about to happen. I went inside the barbershop which is a place that time forgot. Everything about it is redolent of the fifties, from the old-fashioned barber chairs to the razors and combs in their jar of disinfectant. It was like a scene from a Dick Tracy movie. Castro, a Portuguese immigrant, was busy cutting someone's hair in exactly the same way he did twenty years ago when he last cut mine. Despite the two decades since I had last sat in his chair, Castro smiled at me in recognition. I told him what I wanted and he duly obliged. I left his shop sans hair but feeling strangely cleansed. Three years after my recovery, I still visit Castro every ten days to have my hair shaved. I think I do it more to escape the nineties for a few minutes every month than just to keep my hair short.

Minerva Clinic is located in one of those rambling old Victorian houses with creaking wooden floors and high-pressed ceilings almost identical to those in my mother's house. Although the rooms had been converted into wards, I felt as if I was entering someone's home. After the unfeeling sterility of the hospitas in Toronto and Kansas City, Minerva appeared intimate and caring. Even the nurses, both black and white, seemed to handle the patients with more empathy and tenderness. I was shown to my ward which I was to share with three other men who were also undergoing ECT. I lay down on my bed with an unfamiliar sense of calm. At least the treatment which was to follow would be swift. There would be no more excruciatingly long incarcerations or pharmaceutical placebos. What's more, whatever happened was utterly beyond my control. I'd put my life in the hands of a man whom I'd known for less than five hours and I had been forced to take the ultimate leap of faith. Over the next seven days I would either be shocked senseless or jolted back to my senses.

The following morning at about 10 a.m. I was wheeled into the theatre where the ECT would be applied. The last thing I remember before waking up in my bed again around noon was the faces of Brian and the anaesthetist smiling easily down at me before I lost consciousness. There was no after-shock whatsoever. No hangover, no pain, no discomfort. Just a light-headedness and exquisite tiredness, as though every muscle in my body had decided to relax simultaneously. I drifted in and out of sleep for the rest of the day, except that I wasn't sure when I was asleep and when I was awake. The images gliding before my eyes were washed in sepia and sounds seemed to be coming from some far-off place.

At 5.30 p.m., the smell of dinner aroused a voracious hunger in me. I realised I hadn't eaten anything the entire day other than a couple of slices of toast almost twelve hours before. I rose shakily and shuffled the few metres to the dining room which was a converted patio which had been glassed in. The setting sun shone through the windows and the flora of a verdant garden pressed against the panes. The first course was cream of mushroom soup followed by a tough, well-done steak and chips. Dessert was a kind of sponge cake dunked in custard. That night, however, not even Floyd could have prepared a tastier meal. If the first shock treatment did anything, it healed my taste buds.

The third day in Minerva followed the same languid pattern as the second. I spent most of the fourth day dozing, but I recall seeing Hilary's face as though it were through the gauze of a gorgeous dream. In fact, when I think back now, the whole week has an Ariel-like quality to it. On the fifth day I remember Hilary helping me to bath and sharing my table at dinner. I wasn't yet aware of my incipient recovery but even by the fifth day it was dramatic. A severely depressed person is incapable of feeling genuine love for another person because he or she is incapable of loving any part of himself or herself. He or she can only experience the twisted mutations of love like remorse, resentment, anger or guilt. I couldn't yet form my thoughts into words, but when I was with Hilary at that moment, I experienced a spectrum of gratitude, comfort, tenderness and wellbeing through the prism of love.

On the seventh day I awoke at around 9 a.m. I lay in bed for a few minutes before going to the bathroom to wash and shave. It's late, I thought instinctively as I looked at my watch. Time to get up, time to get going, time to make it happen. I went into the bathroom and looked in the mirror. I ran my hand over my face which hadn't been shaved for two days. I turned on the hot water, shaved and rinsed my face. As I looked in the mirror again, I thought to myself: "Hey, Mike, you're not a bad-looking guy at all." I smiled and traced the dimples along my lower cheeks with my fingers. It had been so long since I had seen those dimples I thought they had disappeared. I ran a bath and then eased myself into the steaming water.

As I savoured my warm abandon, I felt a thrill so intense I started to tremble. I realised with a start that I was actually cheerful! I was content! I was happy! I felt great! Out of habit, I reached for my crutch of despair but it wasn't there. My heart began to palpitate as I dared to believe what had happened. I jumped out of the bath and ran dripping into the ward. My exhilaration was as electric as any of the shocks I had received that week. This is unbefuckinglievable, I wanted to scream in ecstasy. Can't be, can't be, can't be, I chanted, not in denial but in wonder. I felt as if I had just had my mental arteries unblocked as my energy flowed furiously back into me.

I dressed hurriedly and ran outside. I inhaled deeply. It had rained the night before and the smell of the wet grass was fresh and rejuvenating. I gazed at the flowers which looked as if they had been illuminated by a subterranean neon light. I listened to the birds which sounded as if they were being orchestrated by some celestial conductor. I saluted the early morning sun as it rose over the koppie and thought: I'm back, I'm back, I'm baaaaaaaaaack! I felt as if everything had been enhanced. My senses felt marvellously alive, as though a black shroud had been removed from them. And that's when I cried for the first time in three years. I sat down on the steps, placed my face in my hands and wept. Long, liberating sobs of relief and thankfulness. The holocaust was over.

"Daddy, Daddy!" Anthony and Carla cried in unison as they ran towards me, their two little faces radiant with expectation. I turned towards them. They were so beautiful! I felt my tears begin to flow again as we hugged each other. "Daddy's better, guys," I said, choking with emotion. "Daddy loves you so much. Daddy's going to make you the happiest children in the world because you're the best children any dad could want. I love you so so so much! You're so beautiful!" We stayed huddled together for awhile before I looked up at Hilary. I could see wonder, incredulity and joy dance about her face. I didn't have to say anything. She could feel my aura. I held her face in my hands and kissed her. She looked so beautiful, she smelt so beautiful, she felt so beautiful, she tasted so beautiful that all I could say over and over again was: "You're so beautiful!"

As Brian promised, it had taken a week to heal me. But there was no guarantee that my health would sustain itself. I was like a prisoner released from a penitentiary. The shock treatment had merely put me back in touch with normality. But like a prisoner released into the world after a long sentence, I would have to relearn how to live and relate to others. The next few months would provide a brutal test of my faith and resilience. I would stumble. I would fall. I would grapple with depression once again and I would almost lose because there is no such thing as a permanent vaccination against depression. There is no pill or treatment that can render the affliction harmless like some strain of polio or smallpox. Each battle with depression is fought face to face, but each victory would make me stronger because it would bring me closer to the truth: the storm is not outside, it's within.

11

Amazing Grace

If you have two slices of bread,
Give one to the poor,
Sell the other,
and buy hyacinths to feed your soul.
MOTHER THERESA

During my final year of depression, my libido leaked from me like water through a sieve. I couldn't bear to be with myself, much less anybody else. My sense of manhood shrivelled with shame and impotence. The disease had castrated me mentally and emotionally, although there were times when I thought it was physical as well. On a more practical level, Hilary didn't allow me near her bed anyway. But the night I came home from Minerva, we slept together as though we were consummating life itself. As it turned out, we were.

Our lack of nocturnal activity during the long years of my depression had motivated Hilary to cease taking contraceptive measures. However, that night of my return to sanity, she assured me that copulation was safe. "I know my body," she said confidently. But as the joke goes: what happens to people who use the rhythm method of contraception? Answer: they become parents.

Five weeks later, Hilary still hadn't had her period. "Don't worry," she said. "I'm often irregular". I was unconvinced and so one night, Lianne Rabner (the person who referred me to Brian just before I was due to enter Tara) and her husband, David, came to us for dinner. After we'd finished the meal, I decided there and then to find out the truth – was Hilary pregnant or not? David and I drove to the nearest day-night pharmacy and bought a pregnancy test. It was one of those tests that required one to mix a few drops of urine with a pink liquid in a little glass vial. If the liquid stayed pink when the urine was added, the test was negative. If it turned transparent then a little foetus was growing. The pharmacist advised us that the test was more than 90 per cent accurate. We bought two tests because Lianne Rabner was going to act as a control. Well, Lee went first. She emerged from the bathroom holding a vial of perfectly pink liquid. Hilary went in and emerged with a vial of liquid clearer than vodka. I still couldn't accept it so we went back to the pharmacy, bought another two tests and repeated the exercise, with the same results. The next day Hilary had the results confirmed by her gynaecologist.

I was strung between terror and delight. It had been less than two months since my recovery. I still wasn't sure whether I could take care of myself, much less become a father to a new little person. I felt the demons begin to encircle me again with their forks of fear and self-doubt. Then I heard Hilary's words: "Mike, this is my dream. All I prayed for while you were making yourself sick in Canada was that one day I would have another baby to love and nurture. Now my dream is coming true. Thank you, my husband, my lover, my friend."

I was also struck by the astonishing timing of the conception, coming as it did on the very night of my recovery. I thought of the miracle of that baby's creation and my recreation occurring on the same day. I realised that self-indulgence was not an option any more. My mother's words echoed in my head: "Think of others and you'll take care of yourself." Celebrate everything you are and everything you have, my spirit commanded me. You are the luckiest human being on the planet. I did, and with that, the demons skulked back into their darkness.

I didn't know it then, but I had just learnt to transform my musings of fear into a self-affirming inner power by doing three things. Firstly, I considered Hilary's wellbeing before my own. Secondly, I changed my focus. By that I mean I concentrated on the miracle of the event, not the crisis that might emerge if I let the demons back into my head. Thirdly, I learnt to neutralise negative thoughts by triggering corresponding thoughts of white light. In the three years since my recovery, these three principles have become ingrained in my psyche. After the initial sting that any setback delivers, I now view every adverse experience as an opportunity to grow and to learn. Because, let's face it, we weren't put on this earth to cruise. We don't grow when things are sailing along. The status quo doesn't force us to introspect and stretch. Life's growth points are carried by bursts of trial and discordance. At these times, we can either choose to creep into a shell of fear and denial, or we can embrace the moment to move forwards and upwards.

Within two weeks of the ECT, under Brian's supervision, I weaned myself off medication. The only pharmaceutical aid I still required was something to dull me to sleep at night. I have found both during my period of depression and the years since then that the hours between 2 a.m. and 4 a.m. are when the demons run rampant. In the days immediately following my recovery, sleep did not come easily. I was too charged to cut the current of energy fueled by the dam break of three years' pent-up passion. And I was not yet strong enough to fend off the fiends alone during that dark time. It would be another month before I could fall asleep at night unaided by sedatives.

When I returned to work at Ogilvy & Mather, I faced an entirely different but equally daunting challenge. Whereas Hilary saw me as a vindication of her faith, my colleagues at Ogilvy & Mather saw a convalescent who had just been through drastic treatment for mental illness. As I walked

133

down the corridor back to my office, I caught people stealing furtive glances in my direction. I laughed to myself, putting myself in their position. I thought of my aberrational behaviour before the ECT. I thought of what I would think if the roles were reversed. I would be cautious about dealing with me or trusting me again. I would also be morbidly fascinated by the concept of shock therapy. I would be curious to find out more about what had really happened to me. I'll tell you all one day, I vowed to myself.

I met with Alan Bunton and Mike Welsford, the managing director of the Ogilvy & Mather Johannesburg office. Both of them were understandably sceptical when I told them I had made a thorough recovery and that I was ready to resume my responsibilities as a senior member of the company. They decided to start me off gently on a small piece of business which was nevertheless important to the company because it was aligned with one of its largest accounts, Volkswagen. For the past year, the account had been spluttering along, but now the clients were demanding a higher standard of performance from the agency. My first assignment was to complete a review of the client's business and recommend a strategy for the year ahead.

I finished a task that should have taken two weeks in two days. My mind raced at warp speed. It was as if the depression and the subsequent ECT had silenced my mind's chitchat, hot-wiring me to my intuition and inner wisdom. I listened to my intuition by being true to myself. I discovered what damage self-deception could wreak and I wasn't going to betray myself again. I had tapped into a source of power that is available within all of us if we sometimes just let go of our fears and allow the divine flair to shine through.

I also learnt to focus totally on the activity I was performing at the moment. I had lived for too long in the past, terrified about tomorrow, when both are really illusions. I realised today was a gift, that's why they call it the present.

Both the client and my colleagues were stunned by the quality of my first assignment. After a few weeks I was given another small client and then a larger one. By May 1992, I was once again running a full portfolio of business. I began to revel in the vibrancy of the South African marketplace. I loved the schizophrenia of this half-breed country, being as it is a paradoxical fusion of sophistication and primitiveness. It mirrored the schism in me. Compared to the silicone, sanitised society of Toronto, Johannesburg's crude energy pulsated off every pavement. More than anything else, though, I related closely with South Africans of all hues. Unlike my outsider status among Canadians, I knew I belonged here. After almost five years away, I found South Africans remarkably open, friendly and hospitable. Despite the labour pains of a new country, there was a level of trust here that was absent in the litigious North American society.

However, my energy flow turned into a swollen river that burst its banks. I was able to handle my own accounts with ease, and so I started making recommendations to management about how to run the rest of the agency, insensitive to their reactions. I also experimented with the way I managed my own accounts in a manner that was out of sync with the Ogilvy & Mather way. To top it all, I took a delight in challenging senior management on almost every issue just for the fun of it. I became a self-appointed maverick whose role it was to fix things even if they weren't broken. I made the serious error of applying the style that had made me so successful at Grey Phillips six years before to my career at Ogilvy & Mather. But they were very different companies with very different cultures.

I felt as if my three years of depression had robbed me of three years' life which I had to make up. Once again, I began to read voraciously. I even got a second job teaching marketing every Saturday morning at the Damelin Management School in downtown Johannesburg. In June, the idea came to me to write about my experience. My motivation was threefold. Firstly, by putting my feelings down on paper

I could understand them better. Secondly, by publishing an account of my experience I would somehow distance myself from the experience itself. My experience would become public domain. I knew that I would undergo a sense of catharsis. I had discovered that the more transparent I was about my depression, the more impotent the demons became. Writing the article would therefore be a kind of public exorcism. Finally, after a few conversations I had with people in the grip of the disease, I knew that I could help its victims by showing them that they were not alone and that the prognosis for their recovery was excellent. But my primary motivation was not to write the article as a service to humanity. It didn't require a great deal of courage. I just felt that it was the right thing to do at the time.

I called *Style* magazine, which I believed had the right profile of audience for the article, and spoke to Hillary Prendini, deputy editor of the magazine. I told her about my idea. She responded favourably, but stated that she had to clear the idea with Marilyn Hattingh, the editor, before giving me the go-ahead. She called me an hour later with an enthusiastic GO! But I almost didn't write it. Some friends of mine told me I was mad to invade my privacy. "Do you really want the whole world to know about your sickness?" they asked. "Do you really want people to look at you knowing that you've been hospitalised for depression? It's the last thing we would do if we were in your position." I vacillated and then decided not to do it. Maybe my friends are right, I thought, although there was still a part of me that wanted to do it irrespective of the consequences. A week before the deadline I called Prendini and told her I had changed my mind, I was backing out. "Absolutely impossible," she shouted back emphatically. "The magazine is about to go to print and we've left seven blank pages for your story. You just cannot let us down."

Whether Prendini was telling me the truth or not, I'll never know, but her pressurised response convinced me that I had no alternative but to write the story if I ever wanted to eat lunch in Sandton again. I wrote the story, and the rest is history. I've written about this little vignette because it illustrates another lesson I've learnt: even eagles need a push. We are all human. We all are prone to hesitation and uncertainty before taking a great leap. But fate conspires to help us if we are truly committed to moving forward. Time and time again, I came to the edge and looked so long before I leapt that I almost didn't leap. Sometimes we have to trust our intuition, have faith and just jump. That's why I love this country so much. Things are happening because they're being made to happen by people who are too naive to know that they can't be done.

By September 1992, however, things had come to a head at Ogilvy & Mather. I was called into the managing director's office where I was issued a warning. I was told that my style was incompatible with that of the agency and that if I wished to keep my job I would have to change the way I conducted myself. Looking back, I understand the agency's stance. I had been with the company for only ten months, the first three months of which I was an invalid whom they carried out of corporate decency. I was barely seven months out of my insanity. And yet I was continuously acting with a chutzpah and audacity that even company veterans didn't dare display.

I didn't heed the warning. I was confident that management would soon see the breakthroughs my actions would generate. They didn't, of course, because I was suffering from delusions of grandeur, which is also a common symptom of bipolar depression. I reached such a manic high that even Hilary began to worry again. Each morning I would wake up swimming in euphoria. I looked forward to the day ahead with a sense of joy and purpose that was almost intoxicating. The difference between my state now, however, and my previous malady was that I didn't come down. I was continuously up. Just when I thought I couldn't feel any better, the next wave of ecstasy would hit and carry me further into Nirvana.

The truth was that I had become acutely conscious of the miracle of my recovery. There was no such thing as the mundane for me any more, only the magic in the mundane. The ability to string two thoughts together; to laugh and make someone else laugh; to cry and make someone else cry; to captivate an audience for just a moment; to have someone invite me to lunch; to be touched by someone in a fleeting gesture of affection; to be liked; to be loved; to be respected; not to evoke feelings of pity or sympathy any more; to feel alive again; to be content. All these things held a thrill that I knew I would never take for granted again. At that early stage of my recovery, though, I hadn't yet learnt how to temper my exhilaration. I hadn't yet learnt moderation. My next life-shattering, life-changing test was less than two months away.

At the beginning of October, my sister called me. "Aileen is dying," she said simply. "She told me her last wish is to see you again before she goes. She wants you to visit her. Mike, I think she's hanging on just to see you. You've got to go see her as soon as you can. I don't think there's much time left." Shortly after I last saw my mother at the end of 1989, she made the decision to emigrate to India. The doctors had given her less than a year to live so she decided she wasn't going to compromise any more. She was going to live her last few months on her terms in her world. She had sold everything in South Africa and emigrated to a town called Vrindaban, about three hundred kilometres north of New Delhi. Vrindaban is one of the holiest places in India because the Indians believe it is the birthplace of Krishna (God). It is also the epicentre of the Hare Krishna movement, to which my mother had devoted the last years of her life. The last time my mother had seen me healthy was in early 1987, almost five-and-a-half years before. I resolved to visit her, and a week later I flew to Bombay where I would take a connecting flight to New Delhi and from there a four-hour taxi ride to Vrindaban. It would be a remarkable, almost religious three-week odyssey that still sustains me today.

138

It assaulted me as soon as I stepped off the plane at Bombay airport – a scorching, suffocating heat. Although it was only 5.35 a.m., it was already 35 degrees Celsius and climbing. I realised I was entering a macabre, alien world when I noticed the rows and rows of corpses lining the streets as the taxi drove me into Bombay. I found out later that they were not corpses at all but some of the over three million inhabitants of Bombay who literally live in the streets. With dawn still a few moments away, I had seen them sleeping, shrouded in their thin white cotton veils. However, if my first day in India had started off strangely, it was to end with an even more bizarre experience.

I was walking down a busy street at dusk when I chanced upon what I believed were three men dressed in drag. As they were beautifully dressed in their silken saris, I asked them if I could photograph them and they obliged. Then, as I prepared to take the shot, one of them lifted up his dress to reveal that he had been castrated. I discovered later that these three men were eunuchs, members of the secret and mysterious caste of the Hijras, which has communities scattered throughout India. These people perform the role of spiritual scapegoats. When a child is born, the Hijras are called in to take on all the sins of the child's past lives. They charge a great deal for their services and no-one dares haggle with them for fear of incurring their curses.

If you take South Africa and multiply it by twenty, you get some idea of the fascination that is India. It is a country about four times the size of South Africa with a population of over 800 million people living in 25 states and speaking twenty different languages. Every year this population increases by approximately seventeen million, more than the entire population of Australia. Like South Africa, India is a fusion of first and third world. It's a land which manufactures rockets and has the most developed software industry outside of Silicon Valley, California, and yet eight out of ten of its inhabitants never travel faster than their oxen can pull their carts. As one Indian said to me: "India is the only country in the world where you choose what century you want to live in."

Bombay itself is the country's commercial engine. To me it was like New York run by God. It's a thriving city of fourteen million people crammed into a narrow finger of land where almost every fragment of pavement is occupied, squatted upon, covered by salesmen, pedlars and homeless families. I thought it must be the only city in the world where people outnumber ants. In fact, the poverty and privation of most of Bombay's inhabitants is so great that Mira Nair, the world-renowned Indian film director who visited South Africa in 1992, stated that compared to Bombay, Soweto is opulent. Yet despite their devastating destitution, I witnessed a gaiety and contentment about them that I found inexplicable. The reason, a wise old man told me later, is that unlike their Western counterparts, Indians have learnt to accept, not expect.

To Indians, in general, religion and philosophy are mother's milk, not just something to be remembered on the occasional weekend or something locked in a book. That's why on almost every street corner there is a shrine sheltering an icon – a beacon of light, joy and hope to punctuate the darkness. Indians live in a state of osmosis with their deities. They believe that invisible forces everywhere act upon them, responding to their every impulse and thought. That's why faith and philosophy are so important, for they are viewed as real powers, not mere abstractions. The crudest statue of God *is* God if one truly believes with all one's heart that it is.

After a few days in Bombay, I went to see my mother. I marvelled at the timing of the trip as I sat in the taxi taking me to Vrindaban. I resonated so intensely with India's culture and beliefs because they corresponded so strongly with the embryonic convictions being formed in my head. We are our thoughts. Our thoughts are the only things that are real, because they guide us towards the choices and decisions that shape our lives. We think what we become.

140

I had proven the power of diseased thinking to myself. Now, I began to understand with elation the force not just of positive thinking but of thoughts influenced and directed by a higher power.

I arrived in Vrindaban at about 3.00 a.m. The taxi dropped me off at the Hare Krishna temple. From there I had a crude map of how to get to my mother's house about half a kilometre away. I wandered down the narrow, dusty side streets winding this way and that until I reached a T-junction near where my mother's house was supposed to be. I paused, not knowing where to go next. It was too early to knock on doors and in Vrindaban there are no such things as street names or numbers. An old man happened by. On the off chance that he might know of my mother, I asked him whether he knew where Arca Vigraha Devi Dasi, as my mother was known in Vrindaban, lived. (Because of the British legacy, almost all Indians can speak at least a rudimentary English.) Before he could answer, I heard a high-pitched, almost schoolgirlish voice cry out from a nearby window: "Mike, is that you? Is that really you?" A few seconds later, she emerged from her house which was no more than ten metres away.

For a minute, we just stood there and looked at each other, unable to believe that we were meeting after all this time in this holiest of places in India. In the three years since I had seen her last, she had become skeletal. I thought that if a gust of wind had blown by, she would have been carried away. Her closely cropped hair was completely white and even her sari seemed to weigh her down. Her face was almost translucent, as though she had already begun the process of travelling from this world to the next. But it was her eyes that riveted me. They were incandescent with joy.

I walked towards her and held her the way one holds a newborn baby, oh so gently and tenderly lest even the smallest pressure causes it discomfort. She was so fragile yet so strong. She felt my quivering emotions and patted me lightly on the back in a delicate gesture of love and reassurance. "Thank you for coming, Michael," she whispered. "My last wish was to see you healthy and happy. You look so wonderful. I've got so much to share with you in the little time God has given us together." Now I was the baby and like a baby that almost loses its breath before it cries, I was enveloped by feelings so intense I almost went into spasm. This was the ultimate fulfilment of our relationship. We both knew that this would be the last time we would ever see each other again. We had fourteen days together to explore a lifetime. I thought of the last time we had met. All I had wanted was for my mother to hold and protect me. Now all I wanted to do was hold and protect her. We had both reached a higher place, but she was nearing the end of her journey, while I was just beginning mine.

It was a singular experience being with my mother in *her* environment. In Johannesburg, she was something of a curiosity with her saffron robes and teelak-painted face. In Vrindaban, however, she was known as "Matajee" (mother) by all who greeted her. In this world, my mother had almost reached saintly status because of the sacrifices she had made and the fact that she was the only woman allowed to come into physical contact with the deities, through her work of painting, retouching and restoring them.

Vrindaban, my mother said to me one day, was not terrestrial, it was celestial. It is believed that even the dust in Vrindaban is divine. You cannot harm a fly in this place because it may embody a sage on its eternal journey back to God. But if Vrindaban was a repository of faith, my mother was a walking miracle. When the doctors in South Africa diagnosed her with terminal cancer in 1989, they gave her no longer than one year to live. Yet here I was with her at the end of 1992. What's more, she would live for over a year more, treated exclusively with Vedic medicine and therapy.

The next few days were immersed in prayers and conversation with my mother. Looking back now, that brief interval purified my spirit. It was where for the first time I made sense of all that had happened to me. I discovered that life is about losing things. I had plummeted into depression because I thought I had lost myself. However, it was a fragile and shallow self that had been lost. I had stayed in depression because I didn't know where I was going or what I wanted to become. I had been immobilised by doubt for three years while I searched for a new purpose and meaning. Now, I distilled my life's purpose for the first time: I would grow and stretch by helping others grow and stretch. I felt as though the force was finally with me.

I was even grateful for my experiences. It was as if I had been given an extra set of senses to savour life. For two weeks, I focused on nothing but how to live a more contented and sharing existence. I learnt that the feeding of the soul is as important as the feeding of the body. In fact, feeding the soul can even sustain the body, as my mother had proved.

One after another, the days seemed to fade away and, before I was ready, it was time to leave the sanctuary of Vrindaban and my mother's company. On our last morning together, she held my face in her hands, and said: "I love you, Michael. Please remember this. My life here is nearing its end. I'm ecstatic, though, that I'm leaving my body here in Vrindaban. My whole life has been successful because of this fact. My body is rapidly deteriorating but I am blissful and God-conscious. I am in physical agony but my focus on the Lord allows me to transcend the pain."

She was silent for a moment as though she wanted to pick the last words she would ever speak to me very carefully. Then she continued slowly and softly: "Please be God-conscious and please make your children God-conscious. This is my only request . . . to cultivate the spiritual life. Please cultivate the spiritual life, then you will all be protected. I love you. Go in peace, live in peace, God bless you." The sound of the hooter of the taxi that was to take me back to New Delhi blared outside. It was time to go. I turned to embrace her for one last time and left. Arca Vigraha Devi Dasi has since left her body, but her presence is alive within me and all the hundreds of people she touched with her amazing grace and faith.

12

Maybe, Just Maybe . . .

And when you're alone, there's a very good chance
you'll meet some things that scare you right out of your
*   pants.*
There are some, down the road between hither and yon,
that can scare you so much you won't want to go on.

But on you will go
though the weather be foul.
On you will go
though your enemies prowl
On you will go
though the Hakken-Kraks howl.
Onward up many a frightening creek,
though your arms may get sore
and your sneakers may leak.

You will come to a place where the streets are not marked.
Some windows are lighted. But mostly they're darked.
A place you could sprain both your elbow and chin!
Do you dare stay out? Do you dare go in?
How much can you lose? How much can you win?
OH, THE PLACES YOU'LL GO! BY DR SEUSS

I returned home with a heightened sensitivity to the potential of South Africa. At the end of October 1992, it wasn't yet the promised land, but it was a land of immense promise. After my time in both Canada and India, two countries as different as night and day, I was convinced that no other place offered the economic and human potential of South Africa. And no other country was as beautiful as this wild, magical land. It was then, and it is now, one of the world's last remaining pioneer societies where the rules are being overhauled and reconstituted as we go along.

Although the recession was still biting deeply, and it would still be another eighteen months before the miraculous events of April 1994, I was pumped with energy and optimism. A sense of certainty and mission had displaced the doubt within me. I had beaten back the bogeyman after almost succumbing to his wiles. Now, I wanted to infect everyone with my enthusiasm. I wanted to make a difference by showing others that fear of self and the unknown was nothing but a phantom that could be vaporised. I wanted to share my new-found belief with all those people who castigated themselves for their shortcomings: the only people who are perfect are those people who celebrate their imperfections. They realise that their imperfections are what make them human and it's their imperfections that offer them the opportunity to grow.

The obvious place for me to begin my mission was Ogilvy & Mather. After all, advertising was all about the communication of a tomorrow that was better than today. It was about possibility, promise, potential, pleasure, and most of all, people. "What if" became my two favourite words. What if we dared to think thoughts that had never been thought before? What if we broke from the past? What if we broke the rules? What if we went to the edge and tried to fly? What if we weren't afraid to be afraid? What if we courted danger as the necessary handmaiden to discovery? What if, what if, what if . . . I wanted to question everything. In a country on the verge of a magnificent revolution, I believed that we had to learn a new way of living and thinking almost from scratch.

The management of the company had a different point of view, however. They saw a man who was being paid to follow orders yet who persisted in thwarting their will and flouting the etiquette of the agency's culture. My behaviour was perceived as an extension of the character flaw that had precipitated my pathology. Looking back, I can't say that I blame them. In terms of traditional measures such as tenure and formal authority, I didn't have the licence to do what I was doing. Furthermore, the agency was highly successful doing business its way. The last thing they believed they needed was a disruptive force in their midst. Over the next few days, the few directors who believed in me would stop me in the corridor or come into my office and warn me to stop non-conforming and toe the party line. The more they told me, though, the more I resolved to be myself. I had learnt one thing during the previous three years and that was to be true to myself, to be true to what I intuitively knew was what I had to do. "Stand your ground," I still thought to myself idealistically, forgetful of my session with the managing director in September, "they'll soon see the the benefits of what you're doing." As it turned out, they never would.

Nine-thirty a.m., 11 November 1992. I was called into the managing director's office. In my persistent naivety, I believed that the objective of the meeting was to finally recognise the wisdom of my actions and even offer me a promotion. The previous two weeks since my return from India had been marked by a number of successes in terms of new ideas sold to clients and growth in revenue from accounts in my portfolio. "Howzit, Mike," I said cheerfully as I bounded into his office after a good meeting with a large account. "We've just sold the new campaign to the Perm. They loved it!" Instead of the favourable reaction I expected, however, Mike Welsford just rose silently and closed the door. Then he sat down and looked at me with a pinched expression. He seemed uneasy as he fidgeted nervously with a piece of paper in front of him. Suddenly I knew I hadn't been invited into his office to be praised or promoted.

"Michael, I regret to have to inform you that we are serving you notice to have you fired," he said in a strained voice. "Over the past three months you have ignored repeated warnings about your conduct in this agency. We think you are a highly talented and ambitious young man but we also don't believe you belong here. We understand the situation you are now in and so we are prepared to offer you a three-month severance package from 1 December. I'm sorry it had to turn out like this but we think it's best for both of us. We will provide you with an office and the agency's facilities to find alternate employment, but you are not to make any further contact with clients. You are also to turn over all your work files and documents to me immediately."

I felt as if I had been hit by a car. Despite the warnings that Welsford had referred to, I never really believed I would be fired. I had thrown myself into my work with almost missionary zeal. Although I knew I was zigging when the rest of the agency was zagging, I always believed that the courage of my convictions would be rewarded. Now I had learnt two more lessons: one, life isn't fair. Two, the perception in my head wasn't necessarily the perception in other people's heads. I just sat there, stunned beyond comprehension. Then fear and rage attacked me simultaneously. The country was still in the grip of a terrible recession. I had just bought a house and incurred debt of over a quarter of a million rand. Hilary was over eight months pregnant. It was the end of the year when no-one was looking to hire new people. I was still only nine months out of my depression. Once word got around that I had been fired, I believed that no other advertising agency in the country would touch me.

The terrible irony, I thought, was that I was in this position only because I had given my work my all and remained true to myself. I was angry at myself, at Ogilvy & Mather, at the world. But most of all, I was scared shitless. What would I tell Hilary who thought that everything was great at work? How would I make a living? How would I ward off the sick feeling of dread and doubt that had instantly reappeared as though by black magic? I implored Welsford to reconsider my termination. I heard myself pleading desperately like a little ten-year old: "I promise you I'll listen to you. I won't misbehave again. Please give me another chance." But he just shook his head wearily and said: "It's too late, Michael. You've gone too far. It wasn't my decision alone to fire you, it's a decision of the board."

I went back to my office, closed the door, opened my drawer and took out my Winstons. Here we go all over again, I thought despondently as I began to chain-smoke again. The earth began to open up beneath me. Once more, the future was black and bleak. All my bravado crumbled as I thought of Hilary's swollen belly and the responsibility it carried. For a brief moment, I almost strangled myself with guilt, thinking about the potential impact my news would have on Hilary's pregnancy. I knew that if I fell down the hole again, it could destroy her and the little life she was nurturing. I resolved not to tell her I had been fired until after she had given birth in about four weeks' time.

That night, on the way home from work, I stopped off at the Radium Beer Hall, a bar about a kilometre from where we lived. As I looked into the bottom of my glass of Scotch, I was struck with the realisation that although I was scared, I wasn't panicking. The shock of the blow I had received that morning had worn off. I was absolutely calm. Instead of wallowing in hopelessness, I began to take responsibility for what had happened to me. I knew that Welsford was right. Not only did I not belong at Ogilvy & Mather, but I had forced them to fire me by constantly questioning their judgement even on routine issues. I thought about the arrogant, abrasive way in which I had confronted my colleagues over the past few months. The memory of my behaviour made me want to cringe with embarrassment.

The righteous indignation that had consumed me the entire day evaporated. It had merely been the inflamed response of my false ego. In its place was the simple but powerful recognition that actions have consequences. I knew then that it was not what happened to me that would determine what came next, but how I coped with what happened to me. "Hey, Mike, this may not be a bad thing," my inner voice said to me. "In fact, you should be grateful. At least you're being paid to the end of February. By then, your baby will be two months old. You know that what happened today was inevitable. It's time for you to walk your talk. If you're such a shit-hot, creative, inspirational dude, go out there and prove it. You don't need to work for somebody else. If you want to go out there and make a difference, start right now. Make your own rules. Maybe, just maybe, you can make it on your own. This is your big test of character. It's too goddamned easy to crumble again. You know you have no alternative. Depression is just a bloody waste of time. And you've wasted enough of that. You can do it, Mike. You know you've got what it takes to go out there and be great. Everything you've been through over the past three years has been preparation for this moment."

I arrived home at about 8.30 p.m. The children were sleeping and Hilary was in the bath. I took off my jacket, unbuttoned my collar and went into the bathroom. "Hi," she smiled glowingly at me. "Quickly, feel here," she said as she motioned me to place my hand on her protuberant stomach. I rolled up my sleeve and touched the side of her abdomen. Sure enough, I could feel the tiny body vibrating within her. I decided then and there to tell Hilary what had happened that morning. I knew that hiding the truth from her would only fester in me like a psychological sore. I hesitated and Hilary looked at me questioningly.

"Hil, I've got something very important to tell you," I said. "It may sound like bad news but I think it could be a blessing in disguise." I paused for a moment as I gathered my composure. Then I said very quietly and deliberately: "I was fired today." I saw the immediate look of shocked disbelief on her face. Before I could continue, she yelled at me: "Why do you always have to choose the hard way? Why can't you just be happy with what you have? At last, everything was perfect. Now the shit has hit the fan again!" She began to cry hysterically. "I'm about to have a baby and now you tell me you're unemployed again. I can't go through it again, Michael. I'm telling you, I can't go through it again."

I had expected Hilary to respond in the way she did. If I were she, I reasoned, I would have acted in exactly the same way. The more agitated she became, the calmer I tried to be. I waited until she had vented her emotions and then I said with as much strength as I could muster: "Hil, this was meant to be. You have to believe me when I tell you that everything is going to be even better than it was before. This is just another test. But it's also an amazing opportunity. This is my chance to prove that I can make it on my own. I know how good I am. I know how strong I am now. I'll never let you down again. And anyway, I'm still going to be paid for another three-and-a-half months. Trust me, my love. After what I've been through, nothing can faze me any more." I reached down and touched her stomach again. "And now, I've got even more motivation to succeed," I said with a reassuring smile. A paragraph from Viktor Frankl's book, *Man's Search for Meaning*, appeared in my mind: *A man who becomes conscious of the responsibility he bears towards a human being who affectionately waits for him, or to an unfinished work, will never be able to throw away his life. He knows the "why" for his existence, and will be able to bear almost any "how".*

In that moment I discovered my "why", in terms of both family and work. I also felt the pride of the small victory within me. This was my first real trial since my recovery. I had begun to fall apart and I had almost immediately pulled myself together. For the first time in my life, I felt the power of an integrated self. I was becoming who I truly wanted to be. Hilary sensed it too because she looked at me through eyes that were still moist with tears and asked: "Is it really going to be okay, Mike? You promise?" "Yes," I nodded emphatically, "it's going to be better than you ever dreamed of." It was only after Hilary went to sleep that I wrestled with the "how" of my future as the Hakken-Kraks prowled and howled around me. But you know what? I made another breakthrough: I realised that it was okay to be scared. It was natural. It was normal. It was human. Courage is not the absence of fear, but the determination to act in the face of it. I decided to use fear not as an enemy but as a friend. Fear was my pathway to growth. As long as I turned into it, I knew that it would serve me well.

It's been just over two years since that night of 11 November 1992. In that time, I have discovered that there are, in fact, two kinds of fear – bad fear and good fear. The bad fear is a disempowering anxiety and worry. It's when we underestimate our own capability to cope with life and overestimate the consequences of what *might* happen if we can't cope. The bad fear drains our strength like a vampire. The phantom problems we conjure up eventually *become* the problem, because the only true reality is the reality inside our heads. The good fear, on the other hand, can energise us. It's the spirit of adventure. It's when we look forward to going where we've never been before. It hones the senses. It's the signal that says we are stretching. I now believe that unless I feel at least a little bit of the good fear every day, I'm not growing. And if I'm not growing, I'm dying. There is no middle ground. So now I'm only comfortable when I'm uncomfortable. I'm only worried when I'm not worried. I'm content only when I'm divinely discontent. The paramount lesson I learnt, however, is that we can choose the flavour of our fear if we become aware of our power of choice.

In the days immediately after my dismissal from Ogilvy & Mather, I resolved to relish my forced sabbatical before the new year. I decided to use the time to contemplate the course of my life and formulate a plan of action starting in January 1993. It was the only time in my life that I devoted myself fully to thinking about both the "why" and the "how" of my future without the myriad distractions of the urgent every-day problems that usually consume us.

In almost all the discussions I've had with highly successful people since, the concept of "time-outs" at life's critical junctures has been cited as the most important process they went through to reprogramme themselves for the next stage of their life's trajectory. Sometimes, to find a solution, we need to remove ourselves mentally and physically from the problem. We need the *time-space* to explore both our options and our feelings about our situation. If we are lucky, like I now believe I was, we have a lot of *time-space* to fine-tune our focus. In the main, though, we are denied that luxury. So we need to create that time-space for ourselves by setting aside small parcels of time throughout the year for reflection, clarification and anticipation.

I also used the time to recondition myself physically. During the dark days of my depression, I visited a faith healer called Michael de Kock. He told me something that I wasn't yet ready to grasp at that stage: exercise, exercise, exercise, because the devil can't stick to someone in motion. Exercise tones the body and cleans the mind. The act of exercise is a mental discipline. My experience convinced me that mind and body are a single unit. If the mind goes bad, the body follows closely behind. Our very thoughts produce different chemical reactions in our body. Every time we laugh, cry, worry, frown, smile, scream, shout, celebrate or curse, we change the body's chemistry. If we indulge in negative thoughts, emotions and actions for too long, we will become sick. One person whom I counselled upset his body's balance so severely during his depression that he became a diabetic. Health, I believe, is a physical state of mind.

On 23 December 1992 at approximately 11 a.m., Dani-Emma Lipkin was born. Weighing in at 3,2 kilograms, with a thick tousled mop of black hair, she was a bundle of miracle, a blessed culmination of a three-and-a-half year journey to hell and back. Somehow, I believe that Dani-Emma knows that she is the embodiment of the entire family's rebirth. There is a light and delight about her that is joy incarnate. Today, at two years old, she is my role model. She experiences life through multisensory encounters. Everything she meets must be tasted, smelt, touched, seen and heard. She lives in a world of never-ending fascination where learning is as natural as breathing. She is pure innocence and naivety. At two years old, she is too young to be cynical, but I pray she retains her sense of wonder forever. Dani-Emma has taught me that babies are astonishing beings. They are the quintessence of the human spirit – joyous, fearless, adventurous, loving, growing. That's why I carry Dani-Emma around with me wherever I go. She is my refuge and inspiration, a walking, talking, bubbling package of possibility.

On 1 January 1993, I gave birth to a baby of a different kind – Touch The Sky (Pty) Ltd, The Imagination Company. During my time-out, I confirmed my belief that I was unemployable. If I was going to make it, therefore, it would have to be on my own. But I didn't want to pigeonhole myself as a specialist in some narrow discipline. So I branded myself as an Imagineer – someone who exploits opportunity through the application of imagination. My mission would be to help people unlock the power of the creativity and courage we all carry around within ourselves to be the best we can be.

I chose the name Touch The Sky (Pty) Ltd for three reasons. Firstly, it expressed what I try to do every day. As Oscar Wilde said: *A person's reach should exceed their grasp, otherwise what's heaven for?* If we keep reaching, we keep renewing ourselves. The moment we achieve our goals, they become merely the launch pad to the next plateau. Secondly, I've learnt the power of words that uplift and inspire us. Today, more than two years since I launched the company, I still feel a thrill every time I look at my letterhead or receive correspondence from someone addressed to Touch The Sky. What's more, after five years in Toronto where a flawlessly blue sky is almost as rare as snow in the Highveld, I still marvel at the perfection from above that greets us almost every day in this country. A blue sky, I once read, is like bread and butter for the soul. The third reason why I chose the name is that it is different and it is somewhat whimsical. It is my way of saying: "Don't take life too seriously, it's too serious for that. Rather, take life passionately. Laugh your way through the turmoil. Cultivate your sense of humour: it can become a lifeline through even the worst adversity."

By the middle of February, two weeks before my last pay cheque from Ogilvy & Mather, I had attracted a roster of clients who provided me with a monthly income almost three times my previous salary. With a wonderful irony, they were attracted to me for precisely the same reason that Ogilvy & Mather fired me. My role in their organisations was to question their existing way of doing things and help them break through into the future by breaking with and breaking out of the past. One of these clients, Reg Lascaris – chairman of the Hunt Lascaris TBWA advertising agency – would become an invaluable partner over the next two years.

Reg is a failed rock star reincarnated as South Africa's most successful adman. He has a captivating, almost teenage candour and spontaneity about him that belies his accomplishments. He arrived in South Africa as a Greek immigrant when he was six years old. Four decades later, despite having built one of the world's most respected advertising agencies, he remains restlessly and happily outside his comfort zone – living proof that it's never too late to have a happy adolescence. I met Reg after my dismissal from Ogilvy & Mather and suggested that we enter into a consultancy relationship. Although my proposed contribution to his business was somewhat vague, we established an immediate empathy that persuaded him to take a leap of faith. That faith was vindicated about six weeks later when I approached him with an idea to co-author a new book about living and doing business in South Africa. Reg had already co-authored two previous best-selling books so he embraced the idea wholeheartedly.

If you remember, the mood in South Africa in early 1993 was still deeply pessimistic. Furthermore, very little had been written about business and life management from a uniquely South African perspective. We decided that there was an opportunity to write a book that would not only give people hope about the potential of South Africa, but also outline the kind of attitudes and actions that were required to thrive in this weird and wonderful place. We called the book *Revelling in the Wild* because South Africa is and will always be wild country. In writing the book, we interviewed hundreds of South Africa's champions of business, politics, academia and the media. What we found was that the two paramount traits that separate the winners from the losers are optimism and passion. In fact, the new champions are passionately optimistic, even when every signal almost forces them into pessimism. In these situations, they are sometimes optimistic simply because the alternative is too horrible to contemplate. But optimism is a learned trait. It's a conditioning of head and heart to search for hope in the most hopeless of situations.

The success of the book exceeded our wildest expectations. Now into its fifth printrun, it was the second-best-selling non-fiction book in South Africa for 1994 after President Nelson Mandela's autobiography. Equally exhilarating for Reg and me, however, was the number of letters we received from South Africans all over the country telling us about the hope and inspiration the book had provided them with. They ranged from a nursery school principal in Port Elizabeth to a social worker in Sandton, all ordinary people doing extra-ordinary things, all part of the Rainbow Nation making the dream the reality.

My story is nearing its end now. But there is one last fulfilment of my dream that I would like to share with you before I close. When I was in my teens, about twenty years ago, I suffered from a severe stutter. I spent my entire life in and out of speech therapists' rooms. In fact, I became so enamoured of them that I eventually married one – Hilary. Slowly I overcame my stutter, although even today I still carry around a slight speech impediment. But, like a physically impaired child who dreams of becoming an athlete, my dream was to become a professional speaker one day.

The opportunity presented itself in the form of an article on professional speakers which I read in the March 1993 issue of *Style* magazine. Ironically, I bought the magazine to read the cover story on lifestyle trends which Reg Lascaris and I had written. As I thumbed through the pages, I came across an article which described the nature of the public-speaking industry and a profile of leading speakers and their agents. I called one of these agents and persuaded her to represent me. I convinced her of my ability and the relevance of my message. She got me my first professional talk on 1 July 1993. It wasn't bad, but it wasn't good. On a number of occasions throughout the one-hour talk, my nervousness made me stutter, much to the discomfort of the audience. Somehow, though, I got another talk and then another. In fact, in the eighteen months from 1 July 1993 to 31 December 1994, I delivered almost two hundred talks and workshops!

My most powerful and gratifying talk, however, was my last one of 1994. It was to a hundred and sixty of the highest performing salespeople of one of South Africa's largest insurance companies. It was also the first time I devoted an entire talk to the story you've just read. I stood up on the stage at a theatre in the Wild Coast Sun Resort and spoke for almost two hours without notes or visual aids. I didn't even have to think. The words flowed straight from my heart and straight from my soul. I took the audience with me on my wild ride of agony and ecstacy. When I cried, I saw the audience crying. When I experienced the thrill of my recovery, I saw them vicariously experiencing it too.

After the talk, I found out why. A number of people came up to me and told me that they felt as if I had been speaking to them alone. They felt as if I was expressing their pain and pleasure. My story, although far more extreme, was their story: the story of what it truly means to be a human being.

Epilogue:

Thank You for Today

Thank you for granting me the privilege of sharing my experience with you. I hope this book has given you at least one insight or realisation that you may not have had prior to reading it. Now, I would like to share some last thoughts with you that I have conceived through my experience. They help me make the most of every day and maybe they will help you also.

- Life is about growth. Growth is about pain but also enormous pleasure – the pleasure of self-discovery and self-realisation. Sometimes, this pleasure is on the far side of short-term pain: growth pain. Don't confuse this vital growth pain with punishment or affliction. Accept it, embrace it, celebrate it. It's a sign that you are moving forward to your date with destiny. Pain and pleasure are Siamese twins. We cannot experience one without the other.

- Crises or problems are merely the midwives of a higher you. They are there to prepare you for the next stage of your journey. Think about it: when do you really grow? When things are going smoothly? When everything is in perfect equilibrium? I don't think so. We grow when we are confronted by the unexpected or the unprecedented. That's when we discover parts of ourselves we never knew existed.

- Depression is often the result of our unwillingness to confront our crises and use them to move forwards. Instead, we allow ourselves to succumb to the bad fear that enfeebles us. From this moment on, I ask you to look again at your life's difficulties. Allow yourself a brief moment of self-indulgent lamentation. That's only human. Then begin finding out how you can use your experience to accelerate your growth and enhance your personal power.

- Remember, there are no such things as coincidence or random occurrences. Everything that happens to us, good or bad, is part of a sequence of events choreographed by a higher logic. We are continually subjected to tests of character. Depending on how we perform, we either progress or slip back to retake our lessons.

- No problem is permanent. "This too shall pass." That's the difference between an optimist and a pessimist. An optimist knows that like life itself, problems are fleeting, mere milestones on life's journey. A pessimist, depleted of hope, is hobbled by his own myopia.

- If you're sometimes confused, that's good. It means you're shedding outmoded beliefs but you haven't yet reached new conclusions. You're in a state of flux. But you're progressing, you're questioning, you're going where you haven't been before.

- Think in terms of "we" and not "me". Only when we constantly remind ourselves of our symbiosis with all other living creatures can we fulfil our spiritual, mental and emotional potential. Symbiosis literally means different organisms living together to their mutual benefit. Be aware of your personal ecology with the people and things around you. In South Africa, this philosophy is also known as *Ubuntu*, a word taken from the idiom *Umuntu ngumuntu ngabantu*: a person is a person because of other people. We are all appendages of each other.

- Live with an abundance mentality and not one of scarcity. Our most vital resources – love, imagination, energy, enthusiasm – are self-replenishing. The more you give, the more you have to give. Think about it: constructive people seem to recharge themselves by their very acts of contribution and charity. Energetic people seem to absorb energy by doing more. By contrast, lethargic, pessimistic or lazy people seem to lose more and more of their life force with each passing moment.

- Tap into the higher energy. Be alert to the wonders of life. My favourite people seem to be eternally naive. They work hard at vaccinating themselves against cynicism. They don't allow the scar tissue of disenchantment to form around themselves. They alchemise their everyday experiences to fire themselves up and energise the people around them. They see the possibility in every situation. In misery, they see hope. In poverty, they see wealth. In the mundane, they see magic. In conflict, they see reconciliation. They know that every day above ground is a great day.

- It's too easy to lose sight of life's real meaning. Too often, we allow ourselves to be distracted by life's sideshows instead of focusing on the main event. The main thing is to keep the main thing the main thing. That's why, right now, I implore you to clarify your own personal mission. Over the next three years, what do you want to achieve? How are you going to grow? How are you going to contribute? What are the values most important to you? Because our values are what determine our behaviour. They are the reason we do what we do. Except that often we don't know what those reasons are because we are not consciously aware of them. The eternal mandate "Know

159

Thyself!" is more relevant today than ever before. If we don't know ourselves, we can't know anybody else. Think about this: who are the people you most like to be with? Aren't they the people who are most comfortable with themselves? Aren't they the people who radiate a sense of balance? By contrast, who are the people you are most uncomfortable with? Are they not the people who are most uncomfortable with themselves?

- We all have a genius inside of us. We are all individual miracles. At the end of our lives, the most important question we have to answer is: were you, you? Or were you trying to be someone or something else? Trust me when I tell you that everyone wrestles with their own demons. Attributes like physical beauty, material wealth or extraordinary intelligence can become their own curse if not handled properly. On the other hand, some of the most powerful people I know have no obvious outward gifts. Rather they have discovered their unique genius and they focus on developing themselves every day to be the best they can be. They have discovered how to love themselves because there is so much to love.

- The first cardinal sin is to hold yourself in contempt, to lambaste yourself for screwing up or making mistakes. People who don't make mistakes usually don't make anything. To make mistakes is be human. Just don't keep making the same mistakes. As my friend Stan Katz says: make mistakes, but for heavens' sake, make new mistakes! Anyway, the past doesn't equal the future. So don't waste time on regret. It's self-indulgent and a hiding place from your obligation to yourself to move forward.

- Know that every word you say to yourself or others, every thought, every action is a step towards heaven or hades. When we deprecate or denigrate another person to their face or behind their backs, we first and foremost demean ourselves. From this moment on, seek to motivate, counsel and uplift others even when you think they've done you wrong. You'll discover an inner power that comes from mastering your own emotions and helping others master theirs.

- Listen, listen, listen. Listen with your eyes, your ears, your heart, your head. Listen to other people's gestures, feelings, words and expressions. The moment we understand why people do what they do, we defuse our own anger or intolerance. We also act with greater effectiveness, because we can go to the cause, not the symptoms.

- Don't be afraid to ask for help. The people who are worth surrounding ourselves with invariably regard it as a privilege to help others. It makes them feel special because being asked for help is the greatest compliment we can be paid. When you're not strong, access a strong person's energy. And know that you will be there for them one day.

- Live life with an attitude of gratitude. When we take nothing for granted, when we whisper thanks for every pleasure, big or small, contentment will follow. Look around you every day and find things to be grateful for. It's the most powerful tonic you can take.

- Finally, be a force for good. Every action we take causes a ripple that joins others to form a tidal wave. Every day, in some little way, make a positive difference. Engage in tiny acts of altruism, make one person smile, feed one hungry person with food or knowledge, pump just one volt of your personal energy into the atmosphere.

I would like to complete our time together by sharing my daily mantra of thanks with you. I read the words which follow every morning to renew and remind me of my faith for the day ahead:

Oh God, thank you for giving me today to make of it what I can.

Thank you for the magic and the miracles that will happen today if I let them.

Thank you for allowing me to feel, to laugh, to share, to cry, to celebrate.

I will be me today. I will listen to my intuition. I will be the best I can be to whoever I meet.

I will face the good things and the bad things that happen to me today with the same gratitude. I know that success and failure are both blessings that lead to breakthroughs.

I will learn, I will grow, I will even try to fly today. But if I stumble, I will get up, steadier and stronger than before.

I will judge no-one today. I will look for the good in everyone today. I would rather be cheated once or twice than live my whole life in fear and suspicion.

I will be fascinated by my life today. I will find wonder in ordinary things because I know there is no ordinary, only extraordinary.

In ways both big and small, I will make a difference today. I am part of the great adventure that is South Africa. Thank you God for giving me this privilege.

No matter what the weather today, I will cultivate my own calm and quietude.

No matter what happens today or what anybody says to me today, I will love myself. Because I know that if I cannot love me, I cannot love anybody.

I will give others more than I take today. I will lift them up through my smile, my words, my actions.

I will only make promises I can and intend to keep today. I know that every time I fail to keep a promise, I fail myself.

I will not allow anger or regret into my heart today. It will only poison me and hurt somebody else.

I will be conscious of my every thought, word and action today. I know I will become what I think, what I say, what I do today.

I will not be afraid of fear today. I will embrace it and use its force to guide me.

I know I will not be given anything I can't handle today, even though it may sometimes seem like it.

I am special, I am wonderful, I am powerful only to the extent that I remember my interdependence with everyone and everything around me today.

Oh God, thank you for giving me today to make of it what I can.